INVITATION
to the THEATER

INVITATION
to the THEATER

by Frank Hurburt O'Hara
and Margueritte Harmon Bro

GREENWOOD PRESS, PUBLISHERS
WESTPORT, CONNECTICUT

*Copyright 1938, 1951 by Harper & Row,
Publishers, New York*

Reprinted with the permission
of Harper & Row, Publishers

First Greenwood Reprinting 1970

Library of Congress Catalogue Card Number 76-109299

SBN 8371-3842-6

Printed in the United States of America

Contents

PART FOUR

Dictionary of Terms and Indexes

Introduction

THIS book is not intended to be the final word about anything. Although it makes some general assumptions, it makes them in a manner intended to leave room for that intelligent dispute which is necessary for the building of vigorous opinion. So we have tried to cover the field of drama comprehensively but in simple terms, aiming to give the gist of a subject as a starting point for individual thinking rather than as a statement of finality.

Probably the first thing that should be said regarding a book about plays is that the reader is twice removed from an actual experience of theater. In reading a play he is once removed and in reading about a play he is once again removed. A play exists only in the moments of its production and to try to enter into an experience of theater with the aid of only a script is a challenge to the imagination; and yet, since a playwright's mind can contrive a play —setting, lines, action, and the multiplicities of characterization— a reader's mind can certainly go far toward reconstructing much of the playwright's intention. The degree of success in this kind of recapitulation depends upon the reader's zest for setting the stage in his own mind and also upon his respect for the playwright's directions and commentary. Some playwrights, such as James M. Barrie, take special pains to bring the reader inside the play, but Barrie was distinctly an actor's playwright. Other playwrights leave a large portion of the directions for setting and acting to the director of the play. When it comes to reading a play we are all directors; as we read we have to bring to the play our share of the creative chemistry that puts a script into production. But then, as part of an audience in a theater we also have to follow the play with our own collaborating imagination, because theater experience is a collaboration of playwright, producer, actor, and audience.

In this book we have tried to take the reader inside the play, to help him feel the playwright's intention as caught up in theme and mood and as expressed through character and action. If we hope thereby to sharpen the playgoer's critical faculties, it is only with the idea of adding to his enjoyment of fine play construction, adept production, and good acting. Yes, and also with the idea that a lively analysis of plays by others may cause the ink to flow from the pen of some shy reader who needs only this added impetus to bring certain characters in his own mind onto their own stage. Our object has been to touch on every phase of playmaking simply but sufficiently, so that the student and teacher and the interested layman generally may be stimulated to further understanding. Thus what we have to say is written in such fashion that the reader may begin to read at any point and go on around the circle in either direction—which does not mean, we hope, that the book lacks method. Rather, that because an individual's point of interest is indeed his own, his method of procedure also is his own. Therefore, the reader may begin with whatever topic answers his current curiosity. Since questions about the drama fall into definite categories, however, we have divided the book into four parts.

The first part presents a discussion of forms of the drama. We have chosen to let the reader begin with the essence of drama as a doing and to let him see this doing amplified and combined with other selected doings into a play. But he may ask almost at once, Why so many kinds of plays? Not so many kinds, really, when one looks closely. Tragedies? Yes, when the central character is completely and grandly defeated. Comedies? Of course, when the perspective that is humor gives equilibrium to an otherwise precarious universe. Farce? Melodrama? Always, when the interest in mere action exceeds the interest in character. And these four basic forms of drama have variations and crossbreedings.

Once the basic lines are laid down, the student soon finds his way, and the first division of this book aims to do this laying down of lines. Drama, the play, its four fundamental forms—tragedy, comedy, farce, melodrama—are discussed both in terms of plays which the reader is likely to know and in terms of other plays which he will enjoy knowing. Then come the many variations of these fundamental forms, varieties as unrelated as heroic tragedy, skit, sentimental comedy, vaudeville. Indeed, the varieties are all here, boldly alphabetized.

The second section of the book discusses structure; that is, how the play is made. The elements of a play need to be understood in their relationships, and are here so presented. Whether one begins as a writer of plays, a producer of plays, or a watcher of plays— whether one is creating understandingly or understanding creatively —the process is much the same. Long before the student has satisfied his interest in even the basic varieties of drama he has discovered that plays have certain things in common and are distinguished by their differences. In any given play, he soon decides whether he is more interested in the characters or in their actions. If his paramount interest is in character, then he is dealing with tragedy or comedy and plunges forthwith into motivation, which is sooner or later expressed in action. If he is more interested in the events that are occurring, then he is dealing with farce or melodrama and finds himself unraveling the plot. But in either case he will be concerned with such technicalities of structure as inciting moment, exciting force, climax, development, denouement, and those elements which together build the finished play. In either case, also, he will deal with suspense and some aspect of plausibility; he will have narration and characterization, both accomplished through many devices. Naturally it is the combination of all the elements that not only makes the play but makes it, through varying emphases, the kind of play it is.

Part Three is a short history of the drama, which we have placed last, after the reader knows enough plays and enough about authors and types to wish to systematize his knowledge a bit for his own enjoyment. We feel that the chances are against a reader's beginning of his own volition with the history of the drama. To teach drama with a broadside of history first is surely a teacher's prerogative and some excellent teachers do so proceed, but it seems to us that in this book to present drama history-first might be to defeat the reader's desire to understand plays in order that he may still further enjoy them. So, history comes last, after the student or any eager-minded inquirer is well inside the art that has enticed his interest. This history gathers up the plays of many countries through many centuries. Not all the important plays are mentioned, but a sufficient number to enable the meticulous student to go on or the blithe amateur to feel that he has a reliable compass.

Part Four includes all reference material. First is a dictionary of all the terms that are used in the book, each term with its own sturdy definition standing alone without the prop of decoration or discussion. These definitions are lifted from the discussions in the first two parts, wherein we aimed to be as specific and concrete as possible, at no point running away from the necessity of setting up definitions—which can then be knocked down. We hope the reader will realize that the purpose of a definition is its service as a point of departure, and will question the definitions on the basis of his own experience with plays. In the process of understanding he may take the book apart and stand up its definitions like a row of tenpins to be shot at, or he may read it like a musical score. We trust he will do the former. Every teacher of the drama or speaker on the drama who has been plied with questions, technical or otherwise, has wished that he might tell his questioners where specifically to find their answers. At least where to find introductory answers. This volume is thus introductory. Although it tells you everything (sic!), it only starts you. Definitions, for the creative, are never an end, merely a beginning.

After the dictionary of terms come the indexes, one of titles, one of authors, and one a general index of subjects. Just as one might suppose, Shakespeare and O'Neill have longer lists of references than some of the esoteric dramatists. The book is made to use, and naturally we find most useful a book which touches our experience at the most points, and most of us, by taste or teaching, are best acquainted with the best-known plays.

Thus our kind of invitation to the theater allows the ticket holder to enter through whichever door he pleases—through the foyer as an attentive spectator, through the stage door as an aspiring participant, up to the desk where the playwright is at work, or even into the historian's archives. The price of his ticket is a measure of his curiosity, an intelligent interest. The best seats are reserved for those who bring also a measure of wonder, which needs no defining for those who have it. But of course when a book is written circle-wise so that a reader may enter at will there is always the possibility that he may walk out of the circle as casually as he entered and begin to make a play of his own. In that case he may never need to come back—although the chances are that in his curious con-templative moments he will do so. And if he does come back, he will probably mentally italicize certain paragraphs and say in sur-prise, "It *is* like that."

Finally, throughout this book in which we invite you to share theater experience with us, there runs the suggestion that it is very nice—we say it wistfully—for the person who teaches drama to know more about drama. We know because we have taught, and we really wrote this volume for ourselves.

F.H.O'H.

M.H.B.

PART ONE

Drama: Essentials and Types

*D*rama

Whether in life, in literature, or upon the stage, drama means exactly what the Greek derivation of the word implies—"a doing." But naturally drama, as we ordinarily use the term, is not just anyone doing anything; it must be someone doing something which is, at least momentarily, significant for the participants.

When the action and the tension are of high significance, we can all see the drama, both objective and subjective, at a glance. Thus when a General Lee meets a General Grant at Appomattox, it is easy to understand the outward drama of a surrender that fashioned history; and it is also easy to sense the inner drama that must have lived in the unspoken thoughts and unexpressed emotions of two such men at such a time. But whenever man meets man drama is implicit. Even the simplest meetings illustrate the possibilities. One small boy, one shovel and a sandpile are not drama, but two small boys, one shovel and a sandpile are almost sure to be. For at once human nature comes into action, and human nature in action is the material out of which drama springs.

We find drama in literature as early as mankind had enough words to tell a story. The story, however primitive, centered about some "doing" which had meaning for someone; otherwise it would never have been selected for telling and retelling. And so drama is always first of all a story, and from the earliest epics to the latest play, drama has shown human nature in action, human beings driven by thought and circumstance. The playwright, like the novelist, merely selects his material from the life about him, from the facts of human behavior and the facets of human character, appro-

3

priating whatever he needs to develop a situation which he has selected. In a sense he does for his selected materials what time and perspective might be expected to do: he brings to the fore the significant. It is this lifting out of its context of less meaningful events that makes a drama, especially a drama as we know it on the stage, because the restrictions of the theater force the playwright to be the most selective of all storytellers.

Not only is this selectivity, this foreshortening, a requirement of the theater but nowhere else is verisimilitude more necessary. The playwright's story acted on a stage is convincing only if he shows characters acting and reacting as we know they act and react in real life. If he swings too far from the ordinary events and persons, he loses the plausibility that persuades his audience that his play is, after all, an interpretation of reality. And yet, to lift verbatim upon the stage the dialogue of everyday, to copy exactly the mannerisms of ordinary people, would be to kill the very thing he is creating— a sense of the essence of life. Therefore, drama has become not only a doing which in its primary experience would arrest the attention, but a redoing which fuses an emotional quality gathered from the expectancy of the audience, the intensity of the players, and the understanding of the playwright.

Drama from its inception had this three-sided participation— audience, actors, and playwright—focusing in an action which, however simple, may be called the play. The hunter home from the chase acting out his swift use of the spear was at once playwright and actor, but even he selected from the series of events as they had happened those which he thought would best convey to his audience of open-mouthed tribesmen the idea of his prowess and success. Nor was his audience a static one; they took up his cries and joined in his pantomime.

Later, as dramatic form began to develop, the same selective process continued along with the same three-sided participation. The community dance and revel which at first had been spontaneous (for the honor and perhaps for the amusement of some genial god) eventually became a planned re-presenting of the more meaningful elements of the festival. The audience, which had at first participated in the acting, now stood apart and participated emotionally, intellectually, and frequently vocally. So too in the drama of sacrifice, of ritual, and of chanted petition, the audience gradually delegated part of their physical participation to their representatives in the person of priest and chorus. All together—audience, actors, and playwright—they developed certain forms for the re-presenting of past experience, of tradition, and of imagined happenings. These dramatic re-presentations were perhaps still produced in honor of the gods, but they were planned also for the edification of the human participants, including the audience.

Thus the playwright, even before he was called by that name, selected the materials for re-presentation; the actors presented the story; and an audience furnished the motivation for the performance. In this simple fashion the drama emerged from the context of life about it. Neither wholly of nor wholly apart from the rest of life, it became an entity in itself—a drama. Or, as we more often speak of it today—a play.

The Play

ALMOST everyone who has ever tried to define the play has arrived at about the same definition: a play is a story presented by actors on a stage before an audience. Each of these three factors has its own importance but it is their combination, so brief in time, that makes the play live. Sometimes we think the playwright the most important of the three because without him there could plainly be no play and his contribution is something we can see, handle and preserve in the archives; but a play is more than a script; it comes to life only in collaboration with actors and audience.

To realize how important are the actors, we have only to remind ourselves how actors can modify a play, changing it intrinsically by the subtleties of their own interpretation, their pacing, even by the timbre of the voice, which is so vibrant a conductor of the actor's own personality behind the personality of the character represented. To an older generation the name Camille brings to mind the Camille of Eleonora Duse or Sarah Bernhardt or Clara Morris, and these are not by any means the same Camille. To recall the names of memorable Hamlets is to evoke a series of different pictures of Hamlet, from the emotional Hamlet of Salvini to the intellectual Hamlet of Forbes-Robertson, and no doubt the original Burbage performance made in effect still another play. Booth was one kind of Hamlet, Barrymore a very different one, and in both cases the action was timed and the actors keyed to the interpretation of the leading character. In recent years Hamlets as diverse as John Gielgud, Leslie Howard, Maurice Evans, and Laurence Olivier provoke in our minds a varied set of responses because each understood and portrayed the play differently. One proof of their difference lies in the necessity each felt to cut or manipulate the text, or to let it stand, in accordance with his own feeling for the play.

Audiences too help to make or to unmake a play. Players know the difference between trying to play to a handful of people and playing to a full house; not only does the full house indicate expectancy and a reputation for success but something sweeps up from the larger group to volatilize the play. However, all full houses are not equivalent. A seasoned road company knows the difference of sectional response in Reading, Raleigh, Butte, and San Francisco; an audience has an emotional and intellectual temperament just as surely as an individual has. Players and playwright do not alone produce the play and Shakespeare is not Shakespeare wherever we find him. There are audiences before whom Shakespeare is much less than Shakespeare and there are audiences—may it be said?—who make Shakespeare what he must have most wished to be.

Just because the combination of play, actors, and audience is so temporary, so impossible of reproduction for purposes of analysis, it is necessary to furnish as best we can the missing elements when we sit apart to contemplate the components that make up successful drama. The script is the only portion of the play upon which we can lay our hands; it is the only one of the three chief factors that remains constant. And so we have to confine our attention largely to a study of the script when we want to try to understand the nature of a play.

However we approach the play, we have to keep coming back to its first essential, which is story, a depicting of somebody's life as it acts upon other lives and is in turn influenced by them. This interplay of lives, which is the essential of drama, may be enriched by the interplay of exterior forces, such as the storm that intensifies Lear's struggle within his human relationships. Or the interaction of individual characters may be complicated by the impingement of social forces which, as in Galsworthy's Strife, become personalized. But whatever the reciprocal actions, a story is the result.

Every play, then, being a story, shows characters in a situation. Every play also has a central thought, whether the playwright knows it or not. And every play has a mood or an atmosphere, because the way the playwright handles his characters and his theme gives the play its mood. Reduced to its simplest terms, a play is characters in a situation, propelled by a thought, enveloped in an atmosphere or mood. Algebraically, Character + Situation + Thought + Atmosphere = a Play.

Having established the fact that plays have certain elements in common, we are at once confronted with the question, Then why are plays so different? They are different because the type of the play grows from the theme, and from the mood the playwright has given to his treatment of the theme. Conceivably themes may be limited in number but there are as many moods as there are playwrights. Mr. Shaw plays with his theme extravagantly, Mr. Galsworthy judiciously, Mr. Barrie lightly, Mr. O'Neill somberly. To illustrate what part the playwright's mood has to do with the development of his theme, one has only to wonder what The Admirable Crichton would have been if Shaw had written it, or Galsworthy, or O'Neill. For this play has a theme which the other playwrights might well have tackled.

Types of plays are so related to and affected by theme and mood that they are not easily described, or circumscribed, but the two basic historical classifications of tragedy and comedy still remain the fundamental types.

Tragedy

A TRAGEDY is a play in which an individual battles with circumstance to his own inevitable defeat. To be sure, something larger than himself, something more meaningful than his own life, may rise triumphantly from his defeat, but as a person he meets the final frustration. In tragedy characters are not mere figures juggled here and there for the sake of plot; they are human beings aware of moral principles, or of inexorable customs, or of natural laws, or even of self-imposed restraints against which their will is impotent. And yet they exert their will. Such basic feelings as fear, hatred, envy, greed, love, pity spend themselves against the specter of defeat; individuals stake all without assurance, so far as their personal desires are concerned; they attempt to manifest faith in something—perhaps their gods, their fellows, or themselves—but without hope. The mood of tragedy may vary from despair to exaltation but the keyword of tragedy is helplessness.

Tragedy used to denote magnitude in thought and emotion, with directness of purpose, tension of will, a sense of inevitable catastrophe, and a linking of individual desires with the larger universal processes. From the ancient Greeks through Shakespeare, and a little beyond, there were accepted absolutes in terms of right and wrong deriving from gods or God against whom individual desires were pitted; the moral principle that triumphed over the protesting individual was accepted by the individual and behind him by both playwright and audience. But with the unfolding of the scientific age, values changed; eternal principles were conceived as social products; "good" and "bad" became less absolute and the individual who broke a natural law or a man-decreed law was seen as himself being a product of laws over which he had slight control. Hence the individual lost some of his individuality, including his stature, in merging with the context of his psychosocial environment, which had furnished his motivations, conditioned his reactions, labeled his sins, and staked out his reward or punishment. The stature of the individual shrank but not the implication of his predicament; grandeur tended to give way to mediocrity but the catastrophe to the individual was not less important. The sense of man amid immensity, which led Brooks Atkinson to call tragedy "the song of man's place in the universe," became not less real but only less well defined.

Aristotle characterized tragedy as the drama of exalted people removed from the realm of common man by their royal prerogatives and the nobility of their estate. Certainly Shakespeare follows this dictum in *King Lear*. Lear is a regal personality; he is built on a grand scale; he has essential dignity of nature. His virtues and his faults are large; he divides his kingdom with a lavish hand; he keeps nothing for himself. He gives generously and he expects unstinted return. We feel that for him to meet defeat is more than the failure of an ordinary individual. In Lear's madness Shakespeare saw

> A sight most pitiful in the meanest wretch,
> Past speaking of in a king.

When Lear's power is reduced to nothing, it is as if fate crushed more than a king and a kingdom.

To be in keeping with the stature of the old king, Lear's suffering must also be on the grand scale. His longing to be loved and cared for by Cordelia is a large emotion, a passionate necessity to his nature. Other misunderstandings and misfortunes are heaped upon him. Wherever he turns he is torn and tortured. And yet— and here is a basic essential of tragedy—the ultimate calamities do not merely "happen" to King Lear. They are the legitimate outcome of actions which spring from character. Lear permitted his wounded vanity to precipitate him into unwarranted anger and rashness. Or perhaps it is more accurate to say that he let a rebuff to his own devotion smother its expression and drive him to express in its place a harshness not genuinely his own. If he had been mad when he gave Cordelia's portion to her undeserving sisters, then there would have been no tragedy. But he was not then mad. He was himself, for good or ill. He started a train of events which, although they grew out of himself, he could not control. And there is the tragic fact of life upon which the tragic play is built, this incalculable racing on of circumstances once they are unleashed by the individual. "The doer must suffer," said the Greeks, and Lear suffers with an intensity impossible had his misfortunes been heaped upon him by a cruel fate. He suffers the calamity of self-realization more poignant than any outward blow.

Lear also shares with the heroes of many other tragedies what might be called the domination of a fixed idea, the identification of his whole being with one passion or one consuming interest. It is this tension of purpose that is a part of the larger-than-mortal plan. Even in tragedies in which a less kingly individual holds the center of interest there is this same tremendous exertion to have one's own way which frequently throws the personality off balance and results in some form of madness.

At the same time the overstraining of the will may call forth magnificent character traits before unrealized. The intense humiliation of Lear before the ingratitude of his two elder daughters brings forth a fine self-control which he had never before been wont to exercise. Qualities he never knew he possessed come up to meet the exigencies of defeat. It is an unknown depth of humility which rises to answer the fool's upbraidings. In repentance, which is really understanding, he accepts indignities with dignity. Through the last part of the play we do not see Lear as deserving the penalties heaped upon him; he has long since wiped out whatever hostages of temperament he gave to fate. He is an acquiescent Lear washed clean of self-consideration. He does not feel the storm on the heath, for his is the complete passivity of the storm's very center. As self he scarcely exists. When he prays he begins, "Poor naked wretches, wheresoe'er you are." His is an awareness of all suffering— a third dimension of experience. He is essentially the tragic human being suffering with the universe an eternal travail. And yet the culmination of the play is a sort of affirmation of the eternal verities; as if age and defeat and the disintegration of achievement only make more sure the regality of the human soul.

The changing centuries have done something to our conception of man's place in the universe. His regality is less a matter of birth and special prerogative; indeed, his meaning may lie in his lack of privilege, in the very fact that he is the common man. If he still seems a larger than mortal figure, it is because he epitomizes humanity. The microcosm speaks for the macrocosm and thus an unimportant individual achieves significance. In tragedy today folk so simple as the women of modern fishermen may make such real tragedy as Synge's *Riders to the Sea*. The faithfulness of their labor, the meeting of the simple necessities of their families without faltering in the face of fear, these have a cosmic dignity. So too is there dignity in the figure of the frustrated Willy Loman in Miller's *Death of a Salesman*. He was never a good salesman but so long as he was physically fit he covered his incompetence from himself by talking loudly to his sons about the principles of success and by constantly reassuring himself that he was "liked." The essential tragedy of his experience lay in his self-discovery, all the more devastating because it was only half clear. To be sure, he had a staggering glimpse of that hour in his past when his own infidelity had killed his son's confidence in him, and at the same time the boy's confidence in himself, but Willy could not see behind his philandering to his need for companionship and fun on his futile sales trips. Accustomed to building himself up in his own esteem, the false figure of himself was more real to him than reality, and the deflating of the figure shattered the fine balance of sanity that is any man's personal adjustment to the facts of his universe. His tragedy was that he could not make his dream world come true and he could not live without his dreams—a predicament of modern man and also the perennial predicament of mankind, born to stand on the earth and reach for the stars. Willy Loman's tragedy speaks for, and to, the defeated within each of us. His suicide is a threat, a warning, but also a regirding for battle. The dignity of his tragedy rests partly in his innocence, his almost childlike unawareness that he has defeated himself. He bemoans his own fate in the loss of his job, control of his sons, prestige with his neighbors, but we cry out against the innocence of ignorance because we sense the shadow figures of the multitude—including ourselves—also skirting oblivion. To Willy Loman death was not the tragedy but only the finality. His true tragedy lay in his meaningless days; nothing in himself nor in his circumstances could possibly free him from frustration. He never knew who he was nor where he was going. In many of the tragedies of our day the chief character is denied the finality of death and left to live on, after the curtain drops, in a round of activity without achievement. Living without hope is harder to bear than death with meaning, and in that sense the contemporary mood breathes despair.

And yet in present-day tragedy there is often meaning behind meaninglessness; we may not altogether understand how a given character reached his particular impasse within the social-economic structure of which he is inextricably a part but we are aware that we too are caught into the same structure and therefore his plight is not foreign to us. We are unhappily involved with him. Today's pity may not be the awed pity that swept a Greek audience as Oedipus went off blinded, but our pity for the frustration of a Loman lifts us beyond our particular brand of self-consideration and so achieves a measure of the catharsis that marked participation in the older tragedies.

Comedy

ALMOST from the beginning there have been two classes of plays, tragedy and comedy. Indeed, in the common mind today that simple classification still prevails. The novice says vaguely, "Tragedies are sad and comedies are funny." The initiate lifts his hand in protest, but in his way the common man is right. For when he says that tragedy is "sad" he really means that it deals with the basic emotions and the primary motivations that are the roots of our being. They are terrifying at times, these roots which push beneath the surface. He draws back, if he can, from their penetration. Full of awe and wonder he reaches for an easy, accustomed word to describe his feeling and he says that tragedy makes him sad. It has always been so. Tragedy and our reaction to it remain the same through the centuries.

And, on the whole, the common man is right about comedy. It *is* funny, using the word broadly again to mean that it appeals to our sense of humor. There are degrees and shades of humor, of course, from the spontaneous sort, which meets a ludicrous situation with a guffaw, to the sympathetic sort, which meets an incongruous situation with a smile. The portrayal of the strictly ludicrous we usually call farce. Actually, comedy began with the ludicrous, which is to say that comedy began as farce. It began with the introduction of buffoonery into the festal procession, or *komos*. Then when tragedy moved from temple to theater, or its early equivalent, these bits of farce likewise marched upon the stage. To relieve the tension in tragedy the playwright early learned to throw in (almost literally to throw in) some comic action unrelated

14

to the purpose of the play and quite dissociated from the stress of character development. Servants, jesters, clowns—anyone would do, just so he performed the antics and made the jests that brought the quick relief of laughter.

But as time went on and plays concerned themselves more and more with ordinary people—or at least with persons who had neither divinity nor kingly estate to magnify the importance of their actions —they began to develop the humor that springs from character. For common men may be as inconsistent as they choose. In fact they have no choice. Given ordinary people acting like themselves (perhaps this is where true comedy begins?), it became less necessary to draw upon the mechanical laughter-provoking devices of farce. Situations took on plausibility and action ran true to its motivation.

In general, we may say that comedy shows character in action through such perspective that the incongruities of the situation touch the humor of the audience. Perhaps "incongruity" might be called the keyword of comedy, for it is the inconsistency of our own natures that keeps us doing the deeds that appear "funny" to others. The real incongruity springs from character. It implies a deviation between aim and accomplishment. All through life most of us are continually trying to adjust ourselves between things as they are and things as we want them to be. In this process of adjustment, our emotions outrun our intelligence (occasionally it is the other way around) and we are, so to speak, jerked out of focus. Of course, whenever we view a moment's catastrophe as an incident suspended in space there is—for us—nothing funny about it; our favorite pipe shattered is our favorite world shattered. But when the catastrophe happens to someone else we see the incident in perspective—the large emotion for the small event—and there is the true humor of incongruity. Just one less pipe in an already smoky world. And the humor has an added flavor when we perceive ourselves in the other person's predicament or, in the rare moments of adulthood, see ourselves in perspective. It is inconsistency that makes us laugh even when the inconsistency is in, and the laugh is on, us.

So the playwright who creates a comedy lets his characters make the mistakes and achieve the successes that produce the incongruous situations. He has no place for the exaggerated motions of farce nor the exterior emotions of melodrama. He does not present action for the sake of action, but action for the sake of expressing character. In melodrama and farce the story becomes both the means and the end; in comedy it is only the means.

In *The Admirable Crichton*, James M. Barrie used situations that might have been farce or melodrama. But he wrote a modern comedy which caused Bernard Shaw to say that it "relegated the old-fashioned nineteenth-century drama to the dustbin." What Shaw must have had in mind was the use of a social theme within a story interesting in itself, a story which grew from real characters and genuine incongruities instead of being built up of the artificial persons and perplexities of the earlier plays.

The basic situation might just as easily have been a situation of farce: tables turned so that a butler becomes the boss through an unlikely shipwreck on a desert island, then the tables turned again so that the butler resumes the old relationship through an equally unlikely rescue of the entire party. Even the incidents of the play might be farce: Lord Loam in London entertaining his servants at tea; the three girls on the island vying for the privilege of waiting upon their erstwhile butler; Lady Mary—no longer languid—dressed in skins, dashing in with a buck across her shoulder, boasting of the way she swam a river "only half a mile broad" to get her shot. On the other hand, the desert island setting might suggest melodrama, as do the fear of wild beasts, the casting into the waves of a bottle containing the story of their plight, and finally the ship arriving to the rescue. Indeed, one could even conceive a possible tragedy evolved from the general situation, but, unlike Lear, Lord Loam leaves his three daughters to worry about themselves while he roams the heath jovially with a homemade concertina.

But *The Admirable Crichton* is ensnared by none of these possibilities. It is comedy. However incongruous the incidents, they are used to bring out the personalities involved; they grow from character. They touch our humor (is it because they touch our experience?) in spite of the fact that few of us have—or are—butlers. When night descends on the island and Crichton, alone by the fire, lifts the lid from the stew so that its savory odors will call home the hungry proud-ones who had left to escape his authority, we know we are seeing comedy. For perhaps, on occasion, we ourselves have retired from the family circle with dignity only to be drawn back by that great leveler of all classes, hunger. And we have a similar sense of comedy when, safely back in London, Lady Mary is once more betrothed to Lord Brocklehurst, who offers Crichton a "place" if Crichton should ever want to make a change. Lord Brocklehurst . . . to Crichton! who had once won the lady on his merits as a man. Through the outward circumstances of the play we sense the humor that springs from character: comedy.

The vitality of comedy consists in a certain timeless quality in the portrayal of follies and incongruities common to all ages. In *The Frogs* Aristophanes satirized his contemporaries but we read the play today and chuckle because it fits so well our own faults and foibles. Molière made hypocrites, misers, and misanthropes walk across the stage with so lifelike a stride that even now we recognize the gait of our own acquaintances. Thus in the particular comedy presents the general, for it presents the particular in such fashion that we feel this thing has occurred before and will occur again. When Mike McInerney, in Lady Gregory's *The Workhouse Ward*, starts throwing things at his crony, we see more than one old man browbeating another to cover up a moment of what he considers to be weak emotion. We see all the blustery old men before and since who would rather be shot down than caught in any act which could even be called sentimental. Because of this particularizing in comedy, this concreteness in presenting the universal through a single individual or incident, we say that comedy catches the occupational gesture; it shows the individual concerned with his task, which is definite, personal, and immediate.

It is here perhaps, in their relationship to the universal, that comedy and tragedy show their basic difference. When we see human nature struggling against inevitable defeat we are seeing tragedy; but when we see it trying to balance itself in the midst of incongruities we are seeing comedy. For the person was right who first said that tragedy shows how men live, comedy how they behave. Since behavior is largely a response to social standards, customs, and attitudes, comedy changes with the times and the people.

Therefore, because it deals with behavior, the values of comedy are not fixed, as the mathematician would say, but are determined at will. Tragedy apprehends as values certain abiding ethical principles. Murder in any generation is likely to be considered a sin against these values. The murders committed by Macbeth in his ruthless contention for power seem as reprehensible to us as they did to his contemporaries. He committed a crime against man and society, and a crime it still remains. But most social standards change, and it is these shifting standards, these "values determined at will," which are likely to be the concern of comedy. The morals of one generation may be modified by the second generation and forgotten by the third. So in succeeding decades certain values may be the subjects of serious comedy, of light comedy, and of farce-comedy. When Ibsen wrote *A Doll's House*, the freedom of woman was a grave question indeed and open to prolonged debate. His play was serious comedy, so serious that some considered it tragedy, but a generation later other playwrights were treating the general theme of woman's rights as light comedy. Women already had their rights, or at least enough of them so that both men and women could afford to relax and laugh. On the other hand, a play which has no serious connotation in one generation may cut deep into the thought of a later generation. When Shakespeare wrote *The Merchant of Venice*, the Elizabethan audience accepted Shylock as a figure of comedy. They laughed at him: he came of an alien race which was the butt of jokes. But the audience of our time sees Shylock as a tragic figure; the psychology of a minority group is one of our significant problems, and even a Shakespeare today would find it difficult to write anything lighter than a serious comedy around such a character.

Thus comedy is probably the most fluid form of drama, ready to be cast in as many molds as there are human predilections. But change as it may with the centuries, it tends to show familiar characters in plausible situations, through them interpreting social conditons and ideas.

All comedy is indeterminate; the action of the play might continue indefinitely, so long as the story held up, because the chief characters of a comedy, even when caught in a serious predicament, are never involved past possible extraction. If Shakespeare had been telling the story of Shylock, the penultimate curtain would probably have been his final curtain, for Shylock was defeated and his tomorrows had no future. But Shakespeare was telling the story of Antonio, as his title implies, and the stories of Portia and Bassanio because they were an intrinsic part of Antonio's story; hence his last act offers a happy solution of the troubles of those characters upon whom he had focused attention. That last act comes almost as a jolt to anyone who today senses the implication of Shylock's situation, but it is the necessary culmination of the essential story of the plot. Culmination? Only in the sense that a pleasantly tangled skein has been untangled and the audience has to go home sometime and might as well go now before another series of interesting incidents presents itself. In much the same way, the closing of the door that shut Nora from her former life was the opening of a door into her new life and the audience knows that Nora is going on about her affairs with characteristic vigor. With the characters of tragedy there is no such projection into the future; a Lear, a Macbeth, and a Loman have no further part in the endless consequences their lives may have set in motion.

Comedy is peculiarly the drama of our own time, the vehicle

of our most serious thought. An age which debunks its heroes has no time for the royal evils nor the majestic virtues that stalked the stage in ancient tragedy. These evils and these virtues do not spring from the life we lead nor the thoughts we think. For the social sciences, including psychology, have given man an awareness of his own motives and an insight into his own environment which restrain him, in the name of common sense, from dealing with great white virtues and great black sins. The numbing fact of two world wars in a single generation has left little chance that an American audience today can accept in the theater the sentimental escapist thrills of an earlier day when sweet melodramas like *Secret Service* and *Shenandoah* were the vogue; nor can we compass even in a tragedy the vast complexity of the world's dilemma. As Yeats remarked to O'Casey after World War I, in a play such a vast picture can be brought to the stage only when reduced to the dimensions of wallpaper in the background. And so, seriously thinking of our greatest problems, we laugh at the personal dilemma of a Sergeant Quirt, or a Mister Roberts, or a collection of sailors, marines, and nurses on a South Pacific island—and, laughing for the moment, do our serious thinking about a subject too large for the solemnities of tragedy.

So also has the appreciation of history lent perspective to modern vision in such fashion that we yield to the inexorable universe only its due and maintain an honest relation with the events of life. We not only see ourselves in relation to the cosmos, but we see the relationship between preceding cultures and our own. Our position on the recurrent spiral of history gives both comprehension of the preceding pattern and some apprehension of what the future pattern will be. Such perspective is, of course, the essence of humor. So Shaw writes *Caesar and Cleopatra* and Sherwood writes *The Road to Rome*. Sometimes we achieve our perspective through a biographical play which presents incidents from the past but selects them with the implications of the present-day political and social scene in mind, as is the case with Sherwood's *Abe Lincoln in*

Illinois and Housman's *Victoria Regina*. To be sure, now and then a modern playwright achieves a tragedy of distinction, but it is more difficult for Eugene O'Neill to write a *Mourning Becomes Electra* for our age than it was for Euripides to write an *Electra* for an age which believed in the ultimate supremacy of its own state and the mingling of gods with men. For the present, serious comedy is a more or less self-conscious attempt at orientation in the scheme of things; it achieves significance without grandeur.

Whether a play is serious or light, we may conclude that there is always comedy whenever the incongruities of the situation move the audience to quick sympathy with the characters and to a humorous appreciation of the difficulties involved.

*F*arce

ALL BLITHE plays are not comedies any more than all debonair youths are in love. When the clothes of comedy are stuffed with too sportive wit and too noisy laughter, the play becomes a farce, which is that special brand of comedy in which logic of plot and development of character are subordinated to ludicrous situations for the purpose of exciting laughter. Situation is the main thing in farce and its people are not really characters but types; people whose general characteristics we know so well that the playwright does not need to individualize them further. Indeed, we might say that farce shows people we know doing things we never dreamed of their doing.

We all know these types—the doctor with slick Vandyke and sparkling spectacles, the professor with baggy trousers and absent mind, the policeman with broad chest and mellow brogue, and so on through the whole catalogue of types. By and large, type characters are the figures of farce because we are keen only to see what the characters will do. Their distinguishing traits are the very traits they must have so that our attention can focus on the predicaments in which they find themselves. The same characters in pure comedy would control the situation. In farce the situation controls them.

Farce is largely a piling up of incidents, exaggerated, impossible, and ludicrous. In real life a man may get himself into an occasional comical situation. In farce he simply slides from one impossible situation to another. We in the audience let him slide: what is a little implausibility among friends? He is generally in trouble or, rather, he thinks he is in trouble, but never the troublesome trouble that needs to trouble us. He generally pretends that he is someone he is not, that he has done something he has not done, or has gone some place where he has never been. His pretense does not spring from character as a rule, but from some situation which compels him to pretend.

It is in this emphasis upon incident rather than upon character that the main difference between farce and comedy lies. In *The Importance of Being Earnest*, Oscar Wilde has used high society characters so typical of the follies of his day as almost to present a comedy of manners. But the ludicrous incidents make it farce. One improbable incident follows another with brave disregard for verisimilitude and the situations have small concern for reasonableness. They are not used to bring out character traits but only to amuse by their ludicrous exaggeration. The very name of the play is drawn from a compounding of ludicrous situations. Gwendolyn adores Jack "passionately" because she thinks his name is Ernest, Cecily loves Algernon because she thinks his name is Ernest. Each man, having faked the name, mitigates the embarrassment of his own shamming by enjoying the other's discomfort —as the audience enjoys the discomfort of both. And then Jack discovers that all his fabrications have been needless for he actually was christened "Ernest" when an infant! And what happened to him as an infant? Why, he was misplaced by his nurse. In a "moment of mental abstraction" she had deposited a manuscript in his perambulator and the baby in her handbag which she forthwith checked at a railway station. And when Jack confronts her with the bag her emotional response is one of calm pleasure that she has her bag restored to her after the inconvenience of being without it for so many years. All this is obviously farce. Near as Mr. Wilde sometimes comes to comedy, he stops short of letting us become interested in his characters as such. With less exaggeration and more plausibility he might have made a comedy. Instead, exactly as he intended, he juggles his hatful of absurdities without once abating his witty patter, and presto! a farce.

Farce has certain devices capable of endless variation. To name them all would be to catalogue the improbabilities. But certain ones are used from generation to generation, always with a betting eye on the chance that there is someone who has never heard them before. And there always is.

There is the device of taking a man out of his element to see how he will act in another element. This device takes the country boy to the city to let him step into a manhole while he gazes at the skyscrapers. Or it takes the city girl to the country, where she frantically climbs fences to escape the mad bull that is only a cow switching flies. Or it takes the eastern dude to the western ranch, where he does not know a cinch strap from a chinch bug. Hoyt's *A Texas Steer* served its decade in America by taking a cattle king to Congress, where his kingly independence does not function so well. Insignificant persons boss him, he has to fight for the privilege of putting on his own clothes. Upstarts bamboozle him out of jobs, kisses, and hundred-dollar bills. When the fellow Texans who are his guests shoot up the hotel as a mere token of good will, he must drag them to safety hidden in bags of mail. However, although he gets himself into trouble, he also gets himself out and the audience laughs twice for each predicament.

There is also the device of mistaken identity. It too is old. When it is based upon physical resemblance, one might suppose that by this time an audience would know all the answers. Shakespeare gave them all in *The Comedy of Errors*. In this single play all the tricks are displayed and there is such rollicking, boisterous confusion between the twin brothers, Antipholus of Ephesus and Antipholus of Syracuse, and between their servants, the twin Dromios, that any lesser confounding of identity seems almost too easy. But, although playwrights of today are wary of the old device, they still use it on occasion.

A favorite variant of this identity device is the confusion built upon someone's being taken for another person who might logically be expected to appear in that place at that time. *Charley's Aunt* and the musicals patterned upon it are illustrations. Charley, in a men's college, is expecting his aunt. He plans to have her chaperon the girls whom he has invited to his dormitory rooms. But a telegram arrives telling of her delay. And almost on the same instant one of his classmates on his way to a rehearsal arrives dressed in woman's clothes. Ergo, the friend will be the aunt. And the aunt he becomes in spite of protestations. And the aunt he remains, although he must listen to all the girls' secrets and refuse proposals from ardent old men. Until, of course, the real aunt arrives and Charley has two aunts on his embarrassed hands.

There is also the device of a man caught in a net of his own weaving. Patelin the lawyer has come down from medieval France to the present day primarily because he got caught in his own trap —ludicrously. Patelin promised, for a price, to defend a shepherd who had stolen a merchant's sheep. On their way to court he coaches the shepherd to act even dumber than he is by answering "Baa," only "Baa," to all accusations and threats. So successful is the stupid "baa" that the case is dropped and the crooked shepherd goes free. But when Patelin tries to collect he gets, instead of money, only another "Baa." Patelin was clever and Patelin was caught—in a ruse of his own devising.

These are some of the standard devices of farce, all still used. There are many other old devices stepping forth in new apparel as jauntily as if they were sallying forth for the first time. It Pays to Advertise presents the father who sets out to teach his son a lesson and instead learns a lesson from the son; Baby Mine portrays the wife who deceives her husband into ridiculous appreciation of the babies she has adopted; Three Men on a Horse shows the meek taking the bit in his teeth and running off with the race; What a Life discloses Henry Aldrich leaping off one hot spot only to land on another, hotter. In You Can't Take It With You an entire family indulge their own hilarious idiosyncrasies with mutual loyalty which makes them all the more formidable to uninitiated callers and would-be in-laws. These modern farces and all their kindred are the old devices although they are dressed for today in at least a semblance of realism.

For even in a farce today's audience demands more plausibility of character than audiences of an older day expected. Today the average one of us is conditioned to conditioning, and even the farcemakers seem to wish to be, vicariously, their brothers' keepers. The characters of their plays perform their antics on the slippery floor of social forces and trip up on the banana peel of a Freudian flaw, as for instance in Mark Reed's *Yes, My Darling Daughter*, or in Moss Hart's *Lady in the Dark*.

Farce not only leans heavily upon human nature as expressed in man's spontaneous response to the ludicrous, but it also takes advantage of his tendency to laugh at someone else's discomfort. To be sure, civilization has largely erased the cruel delight of the savage in his enemy's suffering, for our common life has ceased to make us fear every stranger as a potential threat to security; and we no longer laugh at misfortune. But we laugh when we see people in less serious trouble trying to extricate themselves. We laugh and we feel superior, for we ourselves do not sit in custard pies, or flaunt a roll of counterfeit bills only to find that we are expected to spend them, or absent-mindedly address an invitation to a mother when it is her daughter we wish to dance with. We are above such silly predicaments, but not too far above to be glad it is someone else that is caught.

The dialogue of farce differs from the dialogue of other types in that it is sprinkled with jokes interpolated for the sole purpose of getting a laugh. At their most sophisticated these interpolations are epigrams; at the other extreme they are gags. They are not in either case the amusing comments that grow out of the incongruity of character. Indeed, the gag does not "grow" out of anything. It is not even woven into the fabric of conversation in any real fashion, and to remove it would leave no rent. Rather, the gag is tacked on like a spangle and frequently as a result the dialogue must bear a heavy weight of wisecracks. In *A Texas Steer* someone says, "Red Dog! One of the finest towns in Texas. All it needs is some good society and a little more rain." The answer comes patly, "Some good society and a little more rain? That's all hell needs." The lines may have been original with Mr. Hoyt but a similar gag must have been used to describe a dozen Egyptian towns in the time of the Ptolemies. The gag gets a laugh but it has no special relationship to the theme of the play and is altogether different from the gag programs of the vaudeville stage, or of radio, whereon practitioners like Jack Benny and Bob Hope have developed the apt gag into a fine art which is often, after the laugh is over, a sharp commentary upon the attitudes and mores of our day.

Even when the dialogue of farce has the epigrammatic character-istics of comedy of manners, we realize that the comments make no real difference to—or in—the characters. In *The Importance of Being Earnest* Cecily says that her diary "is simply a very young girl's record of her own thoughts and impressions, and consequently meant for publication." Gwendolyn, instead of Cecily, might have said it about herself and it would fit as well. While we may smile at the frequent epigrams in this farce we feel that they come not out of the characters but out of Oscar Wilde. They are lines for lines' sake. Of course, much of the dialogue in farce, as in any other type of play, simply steps the story forward, but farce adds a lot of sidesteps not at all necessary to the march.

Farce has always been popular when the life of the audience was threatened by some real disaster, as anyone who has lived through a world war knows. During World War I, *A Little Bit of Fluff* played over twelve hundred performances in London while the George M. Cohan brand of exhilaration kept America laughing, but during World War II, in line with the trend to demand more convincing characterization and the verisimilitude of social implication, revivals of Shakespeare's tragedies and contemporary serious plays like Sherwood's *There Shall Be No Night* drew crowded houses both in this country and in bomb-raided London. Does this fact of interest in serious plays even during time of stress mean that farce is on its way out? Not so long as humankind feels desperate to laugh. The blatant farce may go under cover but it reappears, whole or in part, to work the correction through laughter that so enam-oured the Greeks, or merely to offer escape in hilarious portion.

Melodrama

AKIN to farce is melodrama. It also is built of incidents piled upon incidents, but whereas in farce the emphasis is upon the ludicrous, in melodrama it is upon the exciting.

Man has always responded to an exciting story. The first storyteller told exciting stories, no more, no less. (There must have been a first storyteller.) He was out to please his audience, and so with headline technique he got his hero out of one tight place only to get him into a tighter. He needed no subtleties, no highly individualized characters, for his listeners were seeing themselves in place of the hero; they were reliving their big moments or, if they never had any, they were having big moments now in the story, which sped them through hairbreadth adventures. All the excitement and none of the risk! And this, somewhere at some time, was the beginning of melodrama.

Melodrama is a play which grows from situation with emphasis on the involvements of plot and the observance of certain romantic and moral standards. It is primarily exciting. It speeds its incidents and multiplies its difficulties as if trying to see just how many hazards one hero can hold up under and still leave room for a final rescue. Its characters seldom change in any real sense. The good remain good and ultimately receive their just rewards. The bad remain bad—or get worse—and ultimately receive their just deserts. The audience does not need to guess who is going to win, the only speculation is how. The hero is sure to operate well within the rules because melodrama takes no liberties with the accepted standards of the day. Situation, excitement, standards: the three words become a formula.

A deserving young man, about to be made captain of his ship, is accused of taking letters to Napoleon at Elba. One accuser covets his ship and the other covets his girl, while the magistrate who knows him to be innocent holds a grudge against him. He is convicted and sent to a lonely fortress. After twenty years in prison, he learns from a supposedly mad fellow convict of a treasure buried on an island. Whereupon he substitutes himself for a dead man in a gunnysack which is hurled into the sea—and then saves himself and reaches the treasure. Rich, brave and bold, he sets forth to punish those who punished him. The three have become prosperous—a banker, a general, and a magistrate. But he gets his men, one at the end of each act, counting them off as the curtain falls: one! two! and THREE! By the time the final asbestos descends, Edward Dantes, Count of Monte Cristo, has made a place for himself among the immortals of melodrama. He never ignored an excitement nor overlooked a thrill. From a hopeless situation, he worked his way out of each increasingly involved dilemma and kept his actions within the accepted standards of his time.

In another time and another place, there is a handsome, fine, upstanding young lieutenant. Our hero! He discovers that the colonel's lady, in the colonel's absence, is having a rendezvous with a fellow officer. So he goes to the lady's quarters to remonstrate, to save her. While he is there upon his unselfish mission, the colonel unexpectedly returns. The lady, frightened, forces the lieutenant to hide behind the curtains of her window. The colonel, already made jealous of the hero-officer by the villain-officer, finds the noble young man in the ignoble situation. And the young man, in honor, can make no explanation. Situation, excitement, further involvements, until the worthy young lieutenant finally clears himself, reforming the lady with one hand, making the colonel his lifelong debtor with the other, and establishing Augustus Thomas's *Arizona* as a successful melodrama.

Whatever the time or setting, melodrama is primarily interested in situation. *In Old Kentucky* forces its hero into an impasse and then lets the girl save the day, the race, the horse, and the money by herself donning jockey's apparel and riding on to victory. *Secret Service* leads a patriotic spy up to the muzzles of the firing squad only to save him by the heroic intervention of his soldier-brother. *The Shanghai Gesture* takes innocence into the underworld to let it escape at last by the triumph of virtue.

Since melodrama is thus concentrated on situation, it has small time for character. While in many tragedies—*Hamlet* and *Macbeth* are examples coming easily to mind—incident seems piled upon thrilling incident, we note always that the focus is upon character and no matter how close the action approaches the melodramatic, our prime interest is the effect of situation upon character, but in melodrama itself we are absorbed in the situation. The reason is simple enough. The mind of the audience cannot be in two places at once. If the action of the story is as rapid as the eye and ear can take in and the involvements of plot as absorbing as the mind can follow, then there is no mentality left for the weighing of possibilities. So the characters of melodrama are crystallizations and their involvements are not the subjective stress of growth but the difficulties of startling circumstances.

In an older day, for exactly the same reason, melodrama took no liberties with the standards of the day. The weighing of ethical values, which concerned tragedy and comedy, required thought, and melodrama could not spare time for intellectualizing, but instead emphasized especially the observance of romantic and moral standards. These were the gestures of current chivalry. Playwrights wrought their plays out of the material at hand. Pauline, in *The Lady of Lyons*, is sacrificed by her parents to a lowborn dissembler. Eventually her husband confesses his trickery in winning her. She is amazed, she is appalled, she is prostrated. But does she walk out and get herself a job or another husband? Not in Bulwer-Lytton's day. The lofty purity of her love holds fast to her lawful spouse until he, reformed by her nobility, offers his life to France in the thick of the battle. However, after two years he returns home in time, but just in time, to rescue Pauline from the clutches of the villain upon whom she is about to bestow herself in order to save her father from ruin. And then, for fear the audience may still have missed the point, the husband recites the moral neatly in a verse.

That was melodrama in the old days and for the old ways. In our day, if melodrama deals with fewer moral standards it is merely because there are fewer moral standards upon whose validity the audience happens to agree. But if it is less the vicarious morality play, beneath its surface realism it is not less sterotyped; it merely accepts a different set of standards and then goes on creating its excitement within the old pattern.

Originally, melodrama presented a story interspersed with music, as the name would imply (melos, "song"). Songs furnished a considerable part of the sentiment, and instrumental music described and intensified the action. About the middle of the last century music dropped from the average melodrama.

Modern melodrama is distinguished by considerable surface realism, for today the action, setting, and characters all have a certain verisimilitude. One notes, for instance, the surface realism in a melodrama like Archer's The Green Goddess. The story itself is straight melodrama. Major Crispin, his wife Lucilla, and Dr. Traherne, lost in the fastnesses of the Himalayas, are at the mercy of an urbane raja who holds them as hostages against the beheading of his own three brothers in another part of India. There is just enough realism to make the play appear convincing to a modern audience at the time it is being presented. The accouterments of modern life lend a semblance of actuality. Thus the opening dilemma is precipitated by a wrecked airplane, and the final dilemma is resolved by the arrival of a fleet of planes. The bombs, which terrorize into submission the vengeful Indian mob, give the note of the power of science in which modern man finds his measure of security. So the rescue seems possible and the predicament itself is not questioned. The characters also have a surface realism. Lucilla's husband is presented in an unworthy light so that we may have sympathy with Traherne's love for her, but the husband must have some virtue because the all-black villain is no longer convincing. So he is given a last moment's heroism before he is shot by the raja. Perhaps the easy modern dialogue contributes the greatest verisimilitude to this veneer of reality. The talk "sounds so natural" that we accept the characters, plight and all.

One wonders (but not while witnessing the play) what *The Green Goddess* might have been if Archer had utilized a deeper realism and actually started from character instead of situation. Would it have been the tragedy of the raja's maladjustment? Or the serious comedy of Lucilla's loyalty, some part of it belonging to each man? But Mr. Archer wrote melodrama. In the modern manner he achieved his effect by making the situations fairly plausible, the characters fairly credible, and the dialogue tersely of the moment. In these attitudes toward the dress of realism his play marked a transition toward the later play which, although still melodrama, sometimes has so much implication of social meaning that many in an audience miss the fact that they are experiencing melodrama because the excitement of the story coincides with the excitement of their emotional reaction to a social question.

Between the romantic melodrama of the past and the realistic melodrama of the present there have been many variations in form. There was the American variety of the last century, which utilized "local color" characters. A clever ego-satisfaction it was, too, in an epoch when most theater goers could well remember their country origin. Thompson's *The Old Homestead* and Herne's *Shore Acres* shared in this preoccupation with local color. Such plays gave an audience the piquant pleasure of gazing at familiar daily life elevated to the romance of the stage, and perhaps sometimes flattered the audience by letting them see how they themselves had come up in the world. The detective play, of which Gillette's *Sherlock Holmes* was among the first, became melodrama of a more sophisticated form. Its faster tempo was better geared to the increasing speed of its day. Moreover, its intricacy of plot appeals to the research mind trained to recognize no clue as insignificant and no contingency as an impossibility. And it appeals besides to the rest of us who feel we should have made excellent detectives if we had not happened to be something else.

Now when we turn to the current scene for examples of good straight melodrama, we are a bit taken aback to find that the very plays in which melodramatic elements seem most marked do not quite fit the traditional category. Labels which were easy enough to paste on some of the offerings of the classic melodramatists, from Lope de Vega to Bulwer-Lytton and Augustus Thomas, do not fit so well on modern plays of excitement. Pure melodrama is increasingly rare. The current generation, uneducated as well as educated, uncritical as well as critical, demands more than surface realism; we want a psychological realism at least one layer deeper than the trappings of setting and the colloquialisms of dialogue. We insist on asking why the villain and also the hero behave as they do. One of the nagging questions of our day is, How did they get that way? and we apply the question to our political leaders, our neighbors, the members of our families, and even—in our braver moments—to ourselves. In the newspaper, in the picture magazine, on the radio, and on the stage we expect to be informed as to motives not only for the crime but also for heroic deeds. And so even in melodrama, where the deeds matter more than the doer, we look for characterizations more fully drawn than ever would have been necessary in a pre-Freudian, pre-psychosomatic day.

John Steinbeck's *Of Mice and Men* is a case in point. Lennie, the central character, is a subnormal personality, a huge hulk of a man, physically stronger than most, and also tender in a childlike fashion, undiscriminatingly loyal to his friends. With his passion for stroking soft things, he puts his innocent hand on the hair of his boss's wife and then when she screams he shakes her and almost inadvertently breaks her neck because he is afraid his boss might be mad at him and no longer allow him to tend the rabbits. In Lennie's extremity his friend George shoots him to save him from the men who are hunting him down and from the danger of lifelong confinement in some jail. Surely here is the plot of melodrama and also the accouterments of melodrama: night under the stars in the woods by the river; a bunkhouse full of hardened men; a fist fight; a girl of questionable repute; a murder in a stable; a fugitive, a posse, a final homicide. And yet an audience is likely to leave the theater with more feeling for character than for story, and with more feeling for the implications of the story than for the tale itself. Indeed, there is almost a dimension of tragedy in the aggregate of unwanted maladjusted personalities who loom larger than any individual behind pitiable Lennie. In such fashion does present-day melodrama take on some of the perquisites of other forms. Perhaps the best that a critic can do is to say to the would-be labelers that if any given play for them seems to offer its major interest in the characters and what is sometimes called character development, then that play probably falls into the category of tragedy or comedy, but if the involvements of the story itself hold the interest, then the play is likely to be farce or melodrama, and certainly in the latter case, if thrill and exciting incident stand out foremost, the play is melodrama.

Maxwell Anderson's revenge play of today, Winterset, is another in which character interest appears to absorb the onlooker until he pauses to realize that it is actually the juxtaposition of fortuitous incident and exciting adventure that has involved his attention. There is Mio under a bridge, locating the man who can clear the name of his father; there is the gangster who committed the murder for which his father was executed, and a girl who responds to Mio with a love so pure and purifying that it burns out of him the hate that had driven him to seek vindication of a cruelly wronged father and makes him ready to stand unafraid before the gangster's gun instead of seeking escape. These may be convincing characters, but the tragic element is imposed arbitrarily by the playwright and does not grow through inevitability; for most onlookers the unfolding of plot is the attention center of the play and therefore for them the play is melodrama.

In contrast to the melodrama with strong characterization there is the serious comedy with certain melodramatic elements. In *The Little Foxes* Lillian Hellman uses such old devices as a plotted marriage, conniving brothers, a traitorous son, a hounded husband, and yet the plot never overshadows the characters. They have dimension; not only Regina, the strong-minded wife whose will dominates the play, and the daughter, who is like her and also like her more sensitive father, but even ineffectual Birdie, who seems always to be backing into tomorrow with her eyes clinging fondly to yesterday. We could go home from the play and, if we had a mind to, fill in the childhood scenes of every member of the family; we could have done so quite satisfactorily for ourselves even before Miss Hellman wrote *Another Part of the Forest*. Miss Hellman has chosen to create a play about people who are important because they are individuals and if they happen also to be types in a sense and to be caught into arresting circumstances, those facts never outweigh the considerations of motivation and growth, or of that frustration of growth which also stems from character rather than from circumstance.

A greater demand is put upon any present-day dramatist who essays melodrama. He must show how his characters are driven to their acts; he must give them the prejudices and the vocabulary of their time and profession and of their social status; he must hold up ethical standards with which his audience tends to agree. We want all the good things of our self-consciously scientific day but we also want the good things of an earlier day, including unencumbered story for the purpose of excitement. And so we cannot be surprised if now and then we get a mixture which falls somewhat short in dramatic structure and in characterization.

Varieties of the Drama

OF COURSE it would be needlessly didactic to attempt hard and fast classifications of plays. It is impossible to fix every play under a label, to insist that there it belongs and in no other place. While there are certain generalizations, certain types into which plays are grouped, there still remains ample room for that difference of persuasion which makes any art form the subject of variance of opinion. Plays may appear and appeal differently to different generations, to different audiences, to different individuals. Two critics may disagree heartily and soundly as to whether O'Neill's *Anna Christie* is tragedy or comedy, and teachers can—and do—disagree on plays that may seem even less open to question. Classifications may sometimes be useful for study, but surely the playwright writes his play and then lets it fall into what classification it may. However, from time to time the various forms of drama have been given names. Some of these names, such as tragedy, have remained fairly constant in connotation. Others have been modified.

For instance, through the pressure of expanding experience the term comedy has been stretched to make room for attitudes and fashions not within the acquaintance of those who strove for the comedy prizes in the fifth century B.C. Indeed, most of us today when pressed to define the basic forms of drama are likely to speak with reasonable assurance of tragedy, farce, and melodrama, but are inclined to hesitate when we approach comedy. If a play obviously is not a tragedy, not a farce, and not a melodrama, we say, What can it be but a comedy? And, in the main, we are justified in our question and correct in its implied answer. Some form has to mirror the new day and so comedy more or less does it. Modern comedy has concerned itself with the "ends" of life, which were once the province of tragedy, and it has encompassed a variety of the "means" of arriving at those ends, so that we have serious comedies, sentimental comedies, comedies of manners, and other sorts whose very names suggest an emphasis upon some aspect of living.

The term "tragedy" has needed less elasticity because man's apprehension of the tragic facts of life has remained more constant. He realizes today, as he knew in the beginning, that his struggle against a universe which he only partially understands is bound sometimes to prove fatal for the individual. Whether he looks upon his ultimate adversary as fate, or as a conspiracy of events, or as the incalculable elements within his own nature, the fact remains that he faces inevitable defeat when he tries to bend to his own ends certain inexorable laws. And he knows that he faces such defeat. It is the same old tragedy. But, although the tragic element in human experience has a timeless quality, our way of presenting tragedy upon the stage has been modified through the centuries. There are patterns of understanding, and any man in any given age is more or less a part of his day's pattern. His penetration may be as meaningful for future times as for his own, but he expresses that penetration in the language of his time. He has no other vocabulary. So the playwrights of Socrates's day expressed their apprehension of life's tragic significance in one form, the playwrights of Bacon's day expressed their apprehension of the same fact in another form, and the playwrights of every day express themselves in the form best suited to their generation.

ANCIENT CLASSIC TRAGEDY, as we name it now, was written by the Greeks with a respect for form which Aristotle enunciated as embodying the most desirable principles of drama. Structurally the unities of time, place, and action were generally characteristic of this form, although not all Greek plays adhered to these unities. Most of them did so adhere, however, representing events as occurring from sun to sun, within one place, and with no action irrelevant to the plot.

In general theme, this classic tragedy presented the clash between the will of men and the will of the gods. In *Prometheus Bound*, Aeschylus shows Prometheus incurring the anger of Zeus for bringing fire to mankind. Because Prometheus will not bend his will to the will of Zeus, he is chained to a rock where the vultures tear at him perpetually. In *Ajax*, Sophocles shows Ajax claiming the armor of Achilles and setting his will against the will of Athena, who blinds him in order to break his arrogant spirit. In *Hippolytus*, Euripides shows Phaedra demanding the love of Hippolytus in spite of the laws of men and gods, and meeting inevitable frustration. Fate is triumphant in ancient classic tragedy. The will of the gods must be accepted as the moral principle of the universe which brooks no interference.

NEOCLASSIC TRAGEDY. Later European tragedies, particularly the French tragedies of the seventeenth century, written to these same general principles, are usually called neoclassic. The neoclassicists stayed very near to the theme, plot, characterization, and form of the Greek tragedy. To cite illustrations arbitrarily, one might choose from Italy Trissino's *Sofonisba*, from Spain Calderón's *La Vida es Sueno*, and from France Racine's *Phèdre*. The classic pattern persevered until romanticism broke with the unities and admitted a wider range of subject matter and a more spontaneous spirit.

ELIZABETHAN TRAGEDY is a part of the general romantic movement, but it has distinguishing characteristics of its own. In general it discards the unities and departs from the use of classical myths, but it keeps the large central figure whose struggle makes the play. It is still heroic tragedy in the sense that the hero stands out above his fellows with emotions and actions of more consequence than the ordinary man's. Also, it still makes use of the supernatural element. The witches in *Macbeth* are no more to be explained in mortal terms than are the messengers of the gods in classic plays. To be sure, a present-day analyst may see in all injections of the supernatural some objectification of inner need, but certainly such interpretations were not in the minds of the Elizabethans. However, Shakespearean tragedy did show man reaching more deeply into his own nature, searching for his own motivations, less driven by circumstance and more aware of possible self-mastery. Like classic tragedy, it is tragedy on the grand scale, not yet sentimentalized in the manner of the later romantic tragedies, but already reaching toward the psychological motivations of realism.

ROMANTIC TRAGEDY. In a general way, this term may be used to designate the tragedies that broke with the classic, however incidental and accidental such deviation may have been. In sixteenth-century Spain such free-gestured playwrights as Cervantes, Lope de Vega, and Calderón found the garments of classicism too tight for them and so they burst the seams. In liberty's name they took liberties with setting, characterization, form. To be sure, they grew overextravagant but even then it was their own extravagance and not a reworking of the material of the ancients. While the Elizabethan tragedy was the product of romanticism, the typical romantic tragedy as we think of it today comes in a later period. It does not always portray the individual defeated by an eternal moral principle. It holds the attention for its story value and for the mood —romantic mood, of course—in which the story moves. It is really the tragedy of personal adventure wherein the central characters die but leave our thoughts fixed upon the adventure rather than upon the fatal end. If in the end the characters must die, we accept their deaths with a sense of loss but not with the sense of fulfillment through suffering, which is the mark of classic tragedy.

Victor Hugo may be allowed to speak for the romantic tragedy, since it is in his *Hernani* that the romanticists chimed twelve—or maybe thirteen. To read the opening speech is to know the cabalistic touch of romanticism: a hidden stairway, an expected lover, an unexpected villain. To see the final scene is to sense the finality of tragedy; both Hernani and his bride die from drinking the poisoned cup in order that Hernani may redeem his pledge that his life would be forfeit whenever the duke should blow upon his hunter's horn. However, the particular variety of personal honor that Hernani dies to save is based upon the social code of his day rather than upon some underlying ethical principle. There is no sense of cosmic catastrophe in his defeat, no purging of the emotions, no strengthening of the will. Indeed, in our day, to see the play would be only to smile.

TRAGICOMEDY. Somewhat akin to romantic tragedy is tragicomedy, which derives its name from the fact that it averts its own implications by introducing comic incidents and happy endings. It was at first an attempt to dissipate the horrors of gruesome tragedy by relieving the feelings of the audience. Comic characters, who soon became stock characters, were allowed to mingle with the genuinely tragic characters who carried the story. Sometimes the tragic ending implicit in the action was arbitrarily set aside and a happy ending substituted. Such capricious mixing of the tragic and the comic elements tended to produce a false psychology and an artificial construction. Occasionally the playwright might make a fortunate combination of the two components as Shakespeare did in A Winter's Tale. The difficulties in the construction of tragicomedy are apparent in The Merchant of Venice, where the tragic character of Shylock moves behind the triple love stories of the other leading characters but nevertheless looms larger than all of them. The happy ending of the play is expedient for the light characters but inadequate and irrelevant in comparison with the defeat that is Shylock's. Sometimes the mixing of tragic and comic elements was not felicitous but the attempt was a departure, and this drawing together of tragedy and comedy anticipates a modern viewpoint.

MODERN TRAGEDY adds nothing to the essentials of tragedy. While it is free in form, and free in the selection of characters and subject matter, it still deals with the struggle of the individual against forces which will inevitably defeat him. Reflecting the thought of his day, the modern playwright sees man caught in society—a society, paradoxically, which makes him what he is even as he makes society whatever it may be. In the complexities of this society, both sub-jective and objective, man is frequently lost—defeated—as inevi-tably as Oedipus was defeated, or Macbeth, or Lear.

Modern tragedy portrays this defeat. But it does not always allow the central character to die when his defeat is accomplished. It sometimes takes him to a point of departure and there leaves him. The finality may be implicit rather than accomplished. Nor does modern tragedy usually present a large figure as the central char-acter. Kings and those of heroic proportions have given way to com-mon men. That this should be so is simply a characteristic of the times. In this tendency to show an ordinary individual defeated by the ordinary circumstances of which he is a part and then left, per-haps, to live with his defeat, modern tragedy is close to the form of play that we now call a serious comedy. So close, indeed, that some-times it is difficult to state with assurance in which category a play belongs. Thus it is not only to modern tragedy but to modern comedy as well that we may turn for the dramatic presentation of the most serious realities.

Before the advent of nineteenth-century realism the basically serious themes, which dealt with man's ultimate place in his universe and his responsibility to his world, were treated within the framework of tragedy. But the rise of empirical philosophy and the development of the scientific method wrought tremendous changes in man's attitude toward society and toward himself. His verities seemed less sure, or at least they were open to modification. As he looked down the newly opened vista of action and consequence, even his personal defeat and personal achievement appeared less "inevitable." He saw that both defeat and achievement tend to come from within himself and the society of which he is a part. There was a new urge to reckon with the whole of life, with the "good" and the "bad" together, both as valuable aspects of experience.

The modern playwright, then, presents a picture of life which seems real, socially and psychologically, to his audience. We say this realism makes him free but it also curtails him. He cannot fall

back upon the supernatural or upon fate personalized in the will
of the gods, but is confined to the natural order, in its widest
meaning, and his tragedy has a sense of immediacy which the older
tragedy lacked.

Miller's *Death of a Salesman*, Menotti's *The Consul*, and Galsworthy's *Justice* show these modern tendencies. All the characters
in these plays are common folk. In Galsworthy's play, Falder, the
central character, is even weak. He has no overpowering ambition,
no emotions in heroic proportions, no great tension of will. He
never does anything violent. Similarly, there is nothing "bad" about
the men for whom he works or about the men who control the
prison in which he is kept: they are not moved by driving hatred,
or fear, or greed. In none of the characters or in their mingling
together is there "terror and pity" as the Greeks knew these purga-
tive emotions. Falder meets defeat, but it is the social order—that
order of which he is a part—that administers his defeat. We feel
that for him the defeat is final, without recourse. Naturally it is
final after he has killed himself, but the finality was established before the suicide. If he had lived on, there was for him no ultimate
escape from his pattern. Nor is there escape for the other characters.
Each of them, in his own way, is an instrument of the social order.
Riders to the Sea has the same sense of finality. Humble fisher-
folk are completely defeated by the fact that their pattern of life
ties them to the sea. They cannot escape their occupation and
their occupation cannot escape the power of the sea. The finality is
not alone for the men who are drowned but for the women who
live on in their round of work and duty. Heijermans's *The Good
Hope*, with similar theme and setting, shows the finality of ultimate
defeat for men who must work on insecurely built ships, and the
sea, as exploited by the social order, helps to effect final defeat for
its victims.

In some modern plays, defeat lacks this ultimate quality. The
character is thwarted, to be sure, but because society is a fluid thing
and the individual adaptable the audience feels that perhaps the

character may ultimately make a happier adjustment. When this point of view is possible we have, of course, the attitude of serious comedy; the long perspective focused on a far horizon. For instance: Is O'Neill's *Anna Christie* modern tragedy or serious comedy? The story might be either. It is really the story of the weathered seaman Chris who has two passions, mistrust of the "old davil sea" which he could never leave, and love for his daughter Anna, whom he had sent as a child to relatives in Minnesota to get her away from the sea. When she is grown she returns to her father, who sees her still as the innocent girl he sent away, not surmising that the cousins on the farm had betrayed her into a life which makes her mistrust all men. On the barge with her father, the sea seems beneficently to separate her from her past. Then out of the sea comes Matt. Chris perceives the young stoker as a rival and when Matt later wants to marry Anna, the two men fight. The girl, in a desperate sort of honesty, stops the fight with the story of her life in Minnesota. Matt leaves her. Both the man and the girl feel that life has deceived and cheated them, he because the girl was not what he took her to be, she because it could not possibly matter what had happened to her before she knew him. The father, blamed by both, suffers through both. This impasse might have been the culmination of the play—the happiness of all three completely frustrated. But Mr. O'Neill pushes on with the drive of tragedy. Or is it with the indeterminate ongoing of serious comedy? Unknown, each to the other, Chris and Matt both ship on the same vessel. "Old davil sea" at last gets the two men where they cannot avoid each other: "fate" holds them both in its grip. But they are not allowed to die, only— like Anna—to live on.

Is the play a tragedy? Or a serious comedy? The playwright has given it the feel of tragedy, for the story moves in the tragic mood. The characters seem pygmies in a world that is too big for them. They are buffeted by the sea, by circumstances, by their own emotions. Sooner or later they will be crushed. Like most modern plays, *Anna Christie* deals with ordinary persons in a matter-of-fact situation, pursuing their everyday courses toward no high purpose. They meet no catastrophic defeat. They have no fatal end. When the play is finished, life still stretches ahead of them—endlessly.

Most of Mr. O'Neill's plays are tragic in implication. They show man meeting some wall he cannot scale, some hurdle he cannot take. In *Ile*, the captain of the whaler pushes on and on after oil. Something larger than himself drives him forward; he cannot turn back. But his wife cannot go on. Forced to do the thing she cannot do, she loses her sanity. And even after she is insane, the ship proceeds. In *The Hairy Ape* Yank wanted to "belong," to be gathered into the solidarity of that human society to which he had always been a stranger. But he never really belongs anywhere until the tragic moment when he discovers that he comes nearest belonging to the apes in the zoo. In *All God's Chillun Got Wings* the helplessness of mankind as O'Neill sees it is epitomized in the scene between Jim and Ella when she asks if he can ever forgive her and he answers that he can forgive her and she can forgive him—"but how can God forgive Himself!" *Strange Interlude* perceives the same stern tutelage of man: "It's always God the Father when what the world needs is God the Mother." Indeed, the characters in O'Neill's plays, whether in tragedy or in comedy, are forever seeking, and finding at best only temporary answers. *Beyond the Horizon, The Fountain, Marco Millions, Dynamo, Lazarus Laughed, Days Without End, The Iceman Cometh* are peculiarly plays of searching; through faith, through science, through illusion, someone is seeking a final answer, an ultimate meaning.

Modern tragedies present no statuesque figures moving grandly through scenes of magnitude. They show common men; they show the deep uncertainties of human nature. But when the playwright sees his characters going on in a state of imbalance, however serious their situation may be, then he leans toward comedy, for imbalance leaves room for hope.

SERIOUS COMEDY. When Ibsen wrote *A Doll's House* he dealt with life lacking the finality of tragedy, but instead weighted down with the endless implications of the deeds of yesterday and today. He felt the moral obligation of intelligence to be a categorical imperative. That this play is classed by some of the "best authorities" as a serious comedy and by others as a tragedy gives some perception of the new note that had come into drama.

We may define the serious comedy as one which presents a thoughtful theme with characters fully realized; the playwright presents a picture of life as he interprets it, leaving his characters at the close of the play with the same indeterminateness in which we leave our friends at the close of a day. Therefore, few serious comedies come to anything like the standardized "happy ending." They are too close a counterpart of real life for the lyrical culmination. They partake of the current uncertainty that continually challenges the individual's right to take things in his own hands and attempt to work out his personal happiness at the expense of society.

George Kelly's *Craig's Wife* is such a serious comedy. Events conspire to defeat Walter Craig, but they are not events of chance. They spring from character, particularly from the character of his wife. Without his being aware of the process, she is walling him away from his friends and blocking his business advancement. His actions and even his attitudes are misconstrued. He is dominated by his wife, all the more really because his affection has made him blind to the fact. When his aunt, Miss Austen, makes him aware of this slow smothering of his personality, he suddenly sees what life, epitomized by his wife, is doing to him. He must, to save his own integrity, make a complete break with his present setup. He must step out into a future which holds none of the security of home and affection that he had imagined was his. When he finally does go out the door he takes with him the confidence of the audience. Likewise, when his wife is left completely alone after her servants, her relatives, and her friends have found various reasons for departure, the audience feels a stern but almost laughable justice in her predicament. "People who live to themselves, Harriet, are generally left to themselves," the aunt had said. And as the curtain falls she is alone. Thus in his development of the story of Walter Craig's protest against life, Mr. Kelly has followed a general inclination of the modern playwright to present his problem thoughtfully but with perspective, which is the essence of serious comedy.

T. S. Eliot's *The Cocktail Party* is a later example of the thoughtful theme so given perspective that its implication reaches through and beyond the lives of the characters. Essentially Mr. Eliot is dealing with the religious problem of salvation and sometimes he states his problem in religious terminology, although he does so almost parenthetically through the admonition of the psychiatrist. He suggests two answers, achieved at different levels, to the question of ultimate happiness, and then shows the working out of those answers, first through the adjustment of the Chamberlaynes, each to the other and each to himself and herself, and second through the sacrificial death of Celia Coplestone. But, although his theme is serious, indeed philosophical, the characters have the interest, the patter, and the pattern of sophisticated persons, after the Noel Coward manner. Even the character who carries the thoughtful argument of the play, the psychiatrist, is lifted from the context of sophisticated society, and the men and women who consult him do so in the accepted fashion of today; more, the religious interest is a fairly accurate reflection of the degree and kind of interest—and lack of clarity—evidenced when current drawing-room conversation takes a serious turn. Thus does comedy of manners encroach on serious comedy, or serious comedy invade a domain formerly characteristic of the more brittle form of comedy. If the play were considered from the angle of its most daring character, Celia, it might be called a tragedy, for Celia meets death to achieve ultimate meaning, but the play is not Celia's play; it is not the Chamberlaynes' play even though theirs are the lives that have gone from imbalance to equilibrium; it is not the play of Sir Henry Harcourt-Reilly, although it is he who does the maneuvering of the other lives, with the assistance of Julia; it is the play of several lives whose interplay helps to give each of them more significance than any one of them might have achieved alone. At the play's end some of the audience leave the theater with the definite impression that they have witnessed a tragedy; others feel that the play must surely be a comedy with large serious moments; and others, it must be admitted, leave in befuddlement still wondering what the playwright was trying to say.

The thoughtful theme, the indeterminate ending—these characteristics are apparent in such plays as Chekhov's *The Cherry Orchard*, Atlas's *Wednesday's Child*, Emlyn Williams's *The Corn Is Green*, Carroll's *Shadow and Substance*, O'Neill's *Anna Christie*, and Hellman's *The Little Foxes*.

SOCIAL DRAMA. The protest of the individual against circumstances over which he has only partial control has been so much the concern of modern drama, both tragedy and comedy, that certain modern plays are sometimes set apart in a class of their own and are called social drama. The play of protest is likely to be a play directed toward emancipation. Ibsen in *Ghosts* presented the question of the emancipation of the individual from the opinions of others; Hauptmann in *The Weavers* urged the emancipation of the working classes; Shaw in *Widowers' Houses* anticipated the emancipation of the slums from the current landlordism. Other plays in other ways keep on presenting all the other kinds of freedom that obsess and motivate our lives. The social drama, then, may be said to be the play of the ordinary man and his attitude toward the questions of his day. It intensifies social maladjustments by treating them singly, one major difficulty to a play, whereas the novel or treatise is more likely to follow the intricacies of real life, an intertwining of problems.

After the social dramas of Ibsen came a deluge of social and pseudo-social plays. In the midst of the deluge Sydney Grundy coined the phrase "problem plays" to apply to the vogue. He intended the phrase to be wittily disparaging. But it was picked up popularly and subsequently given the accolade of textbook reference.

Propaganda Play. When a play is so given to special pleading that it becomes militant it is, of course, propaganda. It never leaves the audience in doubt as to the playwright's purpose. It piles up documentation to build an emotional effect which shall arouse the audience to thought and if possible to action. If occasionally the playwright can get the audience to proceed from emotion to action without thought he has accomplished his aim more directly.

There are those who feel that the play with an intent to teach or to reform starts with a handicap and seldom overcomes it. When sermon overbalances story, they maintain, a play might as well exchange stage for platform. There are others who maintain that the propaganda play is the theater's best reason for existing, that when the instruction is inherent in the motivation of the characters and the deeds that result the propaganda play is as genuinely drama as any other acted story. When Wexley wrote *They Shall Not Die* he was marshaling propaganda for justice. His thesis is inherent in the title; the incidents build his thesis: Negro youths are browbeaten into admitting a crime they never committed, a girl is maneuvered into accepting gifts for her testimony, a bewildered younger girl is led falsely to confess she is a victim of the crime and then later—aware of the result of her testimony—is led to admit it is perjury. The audience, with the crowd in the courtroom, await the jury's verdict.

The playwright who essays propaganda must expect to be encouraged or condemned according to the temperament of his audience. Plays like Aiken's dramatization of *Uncle Tom's Cabin*, Paul Green and Richard Wright's *Native Son*, Irwin Shaw's *Bury the Dead*, and Odets's *Waiting for Lefty* are all written to the propaganda formula, but at least half the plays we see today have an element of propaganda by indirection.

Didactic Play. All propaganda plays are didactic, because the didactic play is, obviously, the teaching play, the one which definitely aims to instruct the mind or improve the morals. The Greeks used the didactic play, as they used didactic poetry, to gather up the materials of mythology and present them to the audience with something of an authoritative implication, and later the moralities used it in the interest of theology. No doubt the didactic play will continue to perpetuate itself so long as there are causes to be furthered and tenets to be maintained, but the all-time record probably goes to Pratt's *Ten Nights in a Barroom.*

HEROIC COMEDY resembles tragedy, especially romantic tragedy, in its use of at least one character who stands out above his fellows and who carries the adventure that is the play's story. He is a larger-than-average person who achieves greatness through the quality of his nature. Even if he meets final frustration he meets it more gallantly and more philosophically than most. But he is never the truly tragic figure; at all times he is well aware of the incongruities of the successive situations that make up his course of action. This central character is, of course, the hero who makes the comedy heroic. He meets calamities with humor. If he met only one calamity he might be gallant but not heroic. On the other hand, if he met calamities with fortitude minus the humor he might be heroic but he would not be the figure of comedy, for comedy corrects through laughter even when it rises to the heights of sacrifice. So heroic comedy presents the suffering of one who never loses his perspective, who always plays the game with verve even when he realizes the dice are loaded. "One does not fight," as Cyrano puts it, "because there is hope of winning . . . it is much finer to fight when there is no use."

In Cyrano, Rostand presents the figure of heroic comedy at its full stature. Cyrano's life is blighted by a nose—a long nose, a caricature of a nose, a nose which sets him apart from his fellows. If his deformity were more serious, he could not be the figure of comedy, for our pity would outrun our sense of incongruity. As it is, our sympathy is touched with laughter even as his laughter is tinged with suffering. His comments upon his own nose are the braggadocio of one who realizes he is different but does not mean to be defeated by that difference. He fights a duel when the nose is disparaged but even while he fences he composes verses.

There is something heroic, within the romanticism of his day, in Cyrano's refusing to fight Christian when he finds it is the younger man whom Roxane loves. It is comedy when he lends his eloquence to Christian because the young soldier is "dumb in her presence," and comedy again when he diverts de Guiche while the wedding ceremony for Roxane and Christian is being performed. But it is a romantic sort of heroism when he makes his way nightly through the enemy's lines in order that Roxane may not fail to receive her daily letter from her husband. It is comedy when the starving cadets fall upon the hampers of food brought to them in the coach of Roxane. But it is heroism when Cyrano refuses to make known his identity after Christian is killed. Comedy, romanticism, heroism—they are all there in his later weekly visits to Roxane in her convent, in his joking with the nuns about the meat he has eaten on Friday when he has had no food at all, in his coming to Roxane after he is fatally wounded and attempting to give her the news of the day as usual, and finally in his leaning against a tree when he dies, and holding his plume "unblemished and unbent."

There, in the tradition of romanticism, is comedy made heroic. If it seems in the telling more of the theater than of real life, it is nonetheless reasonably convincing in its spontaneity. Heroic comedy is human nature caught, as it must so frequently be caught, in a chain of circumstances not altogether of its forging but neither daunted nor dismayed by defeat.

ROMANTIC COMEDY is the comedy of chivalry and adventure. It persuades the audience that across the footlights wonder is real and the chimerical is the permanent.

Shakespeare knew all about romantic comedy when he wrote As You Like It. The very name suggests the mood. According to our modern viewpoint, the situation is improbable if not downright impossible, but those who do like it say that the improbability is merely a romantic one, and point out that women parading undetected as men were acceptable to audiences acclimated to that particular stage convention. Even today there are many who accept everything that happens in the play as amusing adventure to be enjoyed in the romantic mood. Certainly if Rosalind suffered when Orlando entered the jousts it was a pleasant anxiety, and if the Duke was an outcast he was nonetheless a duke and it was Arcadia to which he was exiled, and the glow of romantic comedy hovers over situations quite outside the experience of any audience.

Similarly romantic is S. N. Behrman's *The Pirate*, which was so successful in production perhaps more because the Lunts are the Lunts than because the adventure is persuasive. In essence *South Pacific* is romantic comedy, as romantic as the illusion we all like to retain of first love on some enchanted evening. In a highly sophisticated way Giraudoux's *Amphitryon 38* is likewise romantic comedy.

The romantic comedy marched down the sixteenth and seventeenth centuries in Spain and then swaggered gaily across nineteenth-century France, Germany, and England to America. Its route is not restricted to any one country nor to any one age. As long as there are repercussions of chivalry there will be answering fanfares from the writers of romantic comedy, because, no matter how earnestly humanity may wear dark shirts for everyday life, it responds to the velvet cloak upon the stage.

COMEDY OF MANNERS. In the generally accepted meaning of the term, the most sophisticated form of comedy is the comedy of manners. In this popular application of the term, it has not changed in essentials since Etherege gave us the first high comedy, *Love in a Tub*, in 1664. Now as then it is the presentation of sophisticated characters in a fairly plausible situation which emphasizes their superficialities and wit by brilliant and satirical lines and generally by at least one high dramatic moment. It is the mirror of society held at such an angle as to catch the foibles of a particular age or set. As a part of the Restoration drama, after the theaters had been dark for nearly three decades, it reflected the manners and attitudes of an aristocracy who indulged in surface emotions and repartee. Even the names of characters in such a comedy as Congreve's *Love for Love* point innuendoes of his day: Scandal, Tattle, Foresight, Miss Prue, Mrs. Frail.

In the earlier comedy of manners the playwright let his imagination play upon a hard surface reflecting a life self-centered or irresponsible and dominated by men and women skilled in intrigue and the artifices of conversation. His play was enlivened by the wily ingenuities of charming women who frequently outwit and overmaneuver the men. His appeal to thought was through the scintillation of the dialogue and the indefinite conclusion. He never drove toward an ethical end, but carried his point by light dissimulation and ridicule.

Perhaps the most typical comedy of manners written by Oscar Wilde, who in a sense may be credited with having revived this form, is *Lady Windermere's Fan*. To begin with, the situation is conceivable—at least if we translate ourselves back to the audience of the nineties. And the characters are as plausible as the situation is conceivable. For the rest, the play goes along with a picture of the foibles and artificialities of the times, held up in strong story interest by a tense situation. It is indeed this tense situation, climbing to a climax, that makes some students of the drama want to call *Lady Windermere's Fan* a melodrama and not a comedy. And in fact the play has the elements of melodrama—it seems to grow from situation and to observe the romantic and moral standards of its day. But all the time the playwright has his tongue in his cheek; he is making fun of the situation. His intention is to satirize, and he bolsters up the satire with a gripping story. His play, then, is comedy of manners.

There is no question of the mood he brings to the treatment of his theme and characters. At no time is his comedic intention more evident than when Mr. Wilde is ready for his "big third-act scene." He stops. He stops to let half a dozen gentlemen pop epigrams about the social order. For this dramatic scene he has let Mrs. Erlynne (who is Lady Windermere's mother although of course

Lady Windermere does not know the relationship) follow her daughter to Lord Darlington's rooms to "save" her. The women hear the approaching men. Lady Windermere is hidden. Mrs. Erlynne then hears the voice of the man who is willing to marry her. She exclaims, "Now indeed all is lost!" or words to that effect, and in her turn hides. Thus far, melodrama. Then the gentlemen file in and promptly begin their verbal sallies.

"Tuppy can't talk about anything but Mrs. Erlynne!"
"Well, that is no business of yours, is it, Cecil?"
"None! That is why it interests me. My own business always bores me. I prefer other people's."

"You want to make her out a wicked woman. She is not!"
"Oh, wicked women bother one. Good women bore one. That is the only difference between them."

"You must leave Mrs. Erlynne alone. You really don't know anything about her, and you're always talking scandal against her."
"My dear Arthur, I never talk scandal. I only talk gossip."
"What is the difference between scandal and gossip?"

And now indeed Mr. Wilde is off to his epigrams. Justifiably, because he is Wilde, the irrepressible spinner of epigrams, and has no intention of letting us think that he is giving us anything except a comedy of manners.

A comedy of manners, if it has vitality, has something of any age as well as its own, but to get its full flavor it should be seen with the background of its own decade. An interesting contrast in periods is the contrast between Pinero's The Gay Lord Quex, first produced in 1899, and Lonsdale's The Last of Mrs. Cheyney, produced in 1925. The difference between the plays is distinct, although they are built on exactly the same "big" situation. In each a comely but desperate woman, confronted by a designing man in a bedroom at midnight, pulls the rope that rings the bell that summons the household, although she knows that she herself will be ruined by her desperate act. Or thinks she knows. Actually, of course, in each case the man gives the play the extra melodramatic twist by shielding the woman and thus saving her. But this situation is the beginning and the end of the resemblance between the two plays. They happen to have the same thrilling scene of melodrama but they are comedies of manners and so each reflects the foibles of its own day. Pinero wrote of a day when all middle-aged bachelors (on the stage) were amiable roués and all maidens needed protection. Lonsdale wrote of a day when "crooks" were fascinating subjects for both audiences and playwrights. Pinero rewards his reformed roué, Lonsdale rewards his reformed nearcrook—with a difference. It is the difference of a quarter of a century. Neither play is to be taken too literally, for each is a comedy of manners.

As in almost all the other classifications, the older definition of comedy of manners needs to be expanded a bit for today so as to take in the greater attention of modern times to the wells of motivation that enrich characterization. Somerset Maugham's *The Circle* is illustrative of this tendency to utilize more fully drawn characters so that the epigrammatic flavor of their conversation is individualized and their wit springs from personal reaction to a situation; nevertheless, it is a sophisticated set that is portrayed and they are caught in a comedic situation which mounts to a high dramatic moment before skidding to a satisfactory if indeterminate resolution.

This comedy-of-manners spirit animates plays like Sheridan's *The School for Scandal*, Barrie's *The Admirable Crichton*, Mitchell's *The New York Idea*, Shaw's *Getting Married*, and Coward's *Private Lives*.

The limitations of the comedy of manners that we have just given, while still so defined by the majority of theater people, are not the limitations set by some others. For there are those who hold that a comedy of manners is a picture of any mode of life which is given by the playwright with sure interpretation and with at least the implication of satire, perhaps by mere exposure. Such definers would include the average play by Molière (others calling these plays comedies of humors instead), and plays like Kirkland's *Tobacco Road* and Odets's *Awake and Sing*.

SENTIMENTAL COMEDY begins at the point furthest removed from comedy of manners. The two forms could not well have less in common and both be comedy. While the manners variety is sophisticated, the sentimental comedy is naïve. It emphasizes the virtue of its characters and the moral quality of its situation, dissipating difficulties by sterling worth, with the underlying suggestion, as in melodrama, that virtue is always effective in an otherwise desperate situation. The formula for this kind of comedy runs much the same through the years. Usually a man and a girl love each other, are kept apart, and are finally reunited. The audience has a double delight: the satisfaction of tears over the lovers' tribulations and the satisfaction of wedding bells at the finish.

The Cinderella story is a perennial favorite among writers of sentimental comedy. It admits many variations without altering the essential fact that a poor girl (or a poor boy) may rise to high estate. In *A Kiss for Cinderella* Barrie lent to the story a mood which separates it from less imaginative adaptations. A common variant of the theme is the character who is thought at first to be of humble origin but proves in the end to be of high estate, as in Manners's *Peg o' My Heart*. Not far from the Cinderella legend is the story of the aristocrat who marries his sweetheart in spite of her humble birth, knowing that her virtues and charm make her his equal in "quality," as the Honorable George D'Alroy did in Robertson's *Caste*. Still another of the almost innumerable variations of this theme is the story of the orphan-ward who marries her bachelor-guardian, as in Webster's *Daddy Long Legs*. Practically all the popular musical comedies used to be cut from the pattern of sentimental comedy, as even titles like *Blossom Time* and *The Student Prince* would show.

Fashions in themes come and go but the sentimental comedy

still appeals to the emotions, as it did when it first came upon the stage in the early eighteenth century. Steele's *The Conscious Lovers* was among the first of the sentimental comedies and was written for a purpose. Steele wished to present a more "moral" attitude toward life than his immediate predecessors had presented in the Restoration drama, which laughed at many standards of the time. Other playwrights, sharing his attitude, took up the new form and succeeded perhaps too well. But if periodically this sort of comedy goes into eclipse, it always reappears and, remaining true to its patronymic, plays to sympathetic audiences—witness *Lilac Time*, *Abie's Irish Rose*, and *The Hasty Heart*.

COMEDY OF INTRIGUE. Between sentimental comedy and the comedy of intrigue, which really antedated the sentimental form, there is the slight similarity that lovers are kept apart, but there is the very large dissimilarity that the comedy of intrigue, instead of observing standards, has none in particular except the standard that the intrigues must be as many and as complicated as the story can use. The comedy of intrigue thrived in sixteenth-century Italy in plays full of treachery, deceit, and scandal. The form had wide vogue in Spain also, and then in France. But the French developed a lighter touch in the "bedroom farce," a considerably modified form of the comedy of intrigue. These plays are not interested in treachery, of course, but their use of gay characters in irresponsible, nonconformist situations lends what resemblance there may be to the early comedy of intrigue. But one seldom if ever classifies a play in this way today.

LIGHT COMEDY. Of all the classifications of comedy, perhaps the most flexible and at the same time one of the most constant is what we call light comedy. Its sole aim is to entertain. But it has a keener sense of individual characterization than farce, demanding a less hilarious response and a more sensitive appreciation. It is volatile, buoyant, even trifling. It may by use of gentle satire or nimble wit appeal to the intellect but not to the point of asking a burdensome thoughtfulness. It merely presents a predominance of pleasant people in a pleasant situation, with swift dialogue moving them toward some satisfactory end. It might be possible to say that O'Neill's *Ah! Wilderness* is such a play. Or is that play a nostalgic comedy of manners of the days of O'Neill's boyhood? At any rate, it is comedy and light. The same might be said of the Lindsay and Crouse plays *Life With Father* and *Life With Mother* or of John Van Druten's *I Remember Mama*. No problem is presented seriously enough to leave the audience in doubt about its outcome and certainly no one need wonder, on his way home, whether or not the solution was ethical. Light comedy is not generically different from other members of the comedy family, only of a livelier disposition. Nor is it confined to any one age or school; the romanticist or the realist, either may handle it as long as he handles it lightly.

In Milne's *Mr. Pim Passes By*, which was so successful in the nineteen-twenties, we know almost at once that Mr. Pim's passing can work nothing but eventual satisfaction for all concerned. The characterizations, the dialogue, the atmosphere are essentially those of light comedy. We know that George's antipathy for Olivia's curtains is only the resentment of a man who will prove tractable in the end. His dismay when he discovers, or thinks he has discovered, that Olivia's former husband is still alive is more diverting than convincing. In fact, all his distresses are calamities built to amuse. Of course, his niece gets her sweetheart and a comfortable allowance along with him; of course, the disturbing former husband is really quite extinct; of course, Olivia gets her curtains, her furniture, her trip to London, and an entirely unnecessary second wedding to a completely devoted George. A comedy whose reason for being is its ability to amuse would not dare any other ending than felicity to all concerned.

Further Classifications

ONE could easily spend too much time to too little profit considering the classifications and varieties of dramatic forms. More and more in modern drama one form steps into the territory of another. Comedy has mingled with farce and the mixture of the two has mingled with melodrama until some of our popular plays may be termed farce-comedy-melodrama. Even a listing of all the names that have been applied to all the forms of drama would take time for no appreciably good end. Nevertheless, because a handy reference may be interesting, even valuable now and then, a remaining miscellany of terms is herewith listed in the only manner feasible for such brevity, which is alphabetically.

A BURLESQUE is a series of dramatic incidents depending primarily upon the use of extravagant images and upon contrast between subject matter and manner of treatment. Trifling questions of the day are presented with mock gravity, or persons of distinction are treated inconsequentially, or works of art are lampooned. It has episodes of staccato dialogue, physical celerity, broad pantomime. In our day the "burlesque show" has minimized the timely aspect and become a composite of farce in the nude, revue in the crude, and haphazard pantomime.

A CANTATA is a story-poem set to music, with the major portion of the story carried by choral arrangements. The music is more lyric and songlike than that for the oratorio. Both cantata and oratorio are accompanied by instruments and usually have more than one movement. The climax of the cantata may be brilliant after the pattern of a light order of fugue.

58

Until the rise of instrumental music in the seventeenth century all serious music was vocal. After the distinction of the sonata as a separate form, the term "cantata" was applied to the religious story sung by one or two solo voices accompanied by the harpsichord and a few other solo instruments. Many of the cantatas of Bach were incorporated as an integral part of the church service. The present-day cantata clings rather closely to a religious theme but makes freer use of nonbiblical texts.

A CHRONICLE PLAY, as its name implies, is one presenting historical characters with incidents chronologically arranged.

This style of play, becoming popular rather suddenly in sixteenth-century England, was a forerunner of the historical play as we know it today. While the modern playwright is likely to use the facts of history merely as a springboard for his treatment of his historical character, the chronicle play began as an epic poem covering the entire life of its hero with only minor incidents invented. The type developed into such a sweeping play as Marlowe's *Edward II* and was expanded by Shakespeare in such plays as *Henry IV* and *Henry V*. Drinkwater's *Abraham Lincoln*, Sherwood's *Abe Lincoln in Illinois*, Eaton and Carb's *Queen Victoria*, Housman's *Victoria Regina*, all use the chronicle method, but seem to view history from the perspective of the present and even to suggest the interpretation of a contemporary thought in the light of past figures. Plays like Shaw's *Saint Joan* and Anderson's *Joan of Lorraine* sound this latter note clearly. A rewarding study of this freer use of historical figures results from comparing Anderson's *Mary of Scotland* with such an older play as Schiller's *Maria Stuart*, or Shaw's *Caesar and Cleopatra* with Shakespeare's *Antony and Cleopatra* and Dryden's *All for Love*.

CLOSET DRAMA, sometimes called LITERARY DRAMA, is written primarily to be read instead of acted. It is usually composed by authors who have distinguished themselves in other fields than the writing of stage plays. Byron, Shelley, Tennyson, Browning, Swinburne wrote plays still read but scarcely ever acted, although

Henry Irving was able to carry Tennyson's *Becket* to some stage success. Among the better-known works of this class are Swinburne's trilogy on *Mary, Queen of Scots*, Bridges's *Prometheus and Hero*, Hardy's *The Dynasts*, and Jeffers's *Tower Beyond Tragedy*. Some closet dramas have poetic sweep but they move best upon the private stage of the reader's mind.

A DANCE DRAMA, obviously, is a story enacted mainly through dancing, whether in ballet or in modern dance.

Thus the ballet is a theatrical form of dance that usually tells a story and as we generally see it might indeed be described as a drama presented in dance form. It has a highly developed technique and is made up partly of classical pantomime to which often are added elements of the more modern dance. In an older day ballets were largely a matter of foot and leg work and if they told a story at all it was a pretty story and likely to have as *dramatis personae* the fanciful figures of elfland. But the whole aspect has changed in modern times and particularly on the contemporary stage. The ballet now is characterized by a dramatic projection which seems almost limitless in possibilities.

The first ballet as a combination of dancing and music for the display of coherent dramatic idea was sponsored by Catherine de Médicis, who had brought the general idea to France from Italy. The next step in its development came in the reign of Louis XIV when Pierre Beauchamps perfected the five basic foot positions from which all later ballet technique stemmed. From the seventeenth century through the nineteenth the center of ballet influence fluctuated between France and Italy, but at the beginning of the twentieth century it shifted to Russia, where an imperial school had been established under the direction of French and Italian masters. The development in Russia was rapid and spectacular. Many teachers, choreographers, dancers, and musicians worked together to achieve the finest ballet the world had yet known. To think of this era is to recall such names as Pavlova, Karsavina, Nijinsky, Bolm, Mordkin, Massine, and many others. The prolific choreographers included Petipa, and later Fokine and Diaghilev.

It was after the Russian revolution that America and England began to develop the training of ballet dancers, chiefly because Russian artists seeking refuge began to enter the profession of teaching in addition to dancing. Today the English-speaking nations are making their own distinctive contributions, in England notably by the Sadler's Wells company, subsidized by the British government, animated by the zeal of Ninette de Valois, and featuring such dancers as Margot Fonteyn, Robert Helpmann, Moira Shearer, Michael Somes, and Beryl Grey. In the United States there are three major ballet companies: the Ballet Russe, which has survived several changes since the initial company was formed by René Blum and Colonel de Basil; the Ballet Theatre, founded by Lucia Chase; and the New York City Ballet, headed by Lincoln Kirstein. Among the choreographers of recent years are Georges Balanchine, Antony Tudor, Leonide Massine, Frederick Ashton, and Ruth Page, and the dancers include Alexandra Danilova, Alicia Markova, Nana Gollner, Nora Kaye, Alicia Alonso, Igor Youskevitch, André Eglevsky, Frederic Franklin, John Kriza, Hugh Laing and Bentley Stone.

An important stage in the popularization of the ballet came with its introduction into the big Broadway musicals. Beginning with Agnes De Mille's modern ballets in *Oklahoma* in 1943, this form of the dance became as important as the songs in such productions as this one and *Bloomer Girl, Carousel, Allegro,* and *Look, Ma, I'm Dancin'.* These ballets departed somewhat from the classical pattern, adding a modern note to the older form, and most students of the dance feel that this intermingling of the new with the old has been good for both. No better indication of the extent to which ballet has become a popular part of our theater fare need be given than to remark its advent not only into musicals but also into the cinema in such films as *The Red Shoes, Louisiana Purchase,* and *Spanish Fiesta,* featuring artists with the ballet background of Moira Shearer, Vera Zorina, Jack Cole, George Zoritch, and others. Indeed, what with the coming of the ballet to the screen, along with such diversified numbers as those by Fred Astaire,

Ray Bolger, Ginger Rogers, and Gene Kelly, the dance has become an importantly popular feature of many motion pictures; and when one adds to this fact the fact also that what is sometimes called modern dance is seen increasingly in theaters and on the concert stage one can appreciate how general is the acceptance of dance as a part of dramatic entertainment today.

From earliest times man has enjoyed rhythmical movement of feet and body and in his very early stages found pantomime the natural means of conveying emotions and ideas. So the origin of the dramatic dance is no different from the origin of drama in any other form. Nowhere is this fact more clearly seen than in what is called modern dance, although the term "modern" is really a misnomer, inasmuch as the object of its original exponents was to go back to the primitive method of expressing emotions per se, neither representationally nor narratively. It was Isadora Duncan who first, in the nineties, introduced this so-called modern dance. Among others to advance the art have been Ruth St. Denis, Mary Wigman, Ted Shawn, Doris Humphrey, Martha Graham, Charles Weidman, Hanya Holm, Helen Tamiris, José Limon, Katherine Dunham, Pearl Primus, Valerie Bettis, Jane Dudley, Sophie Maslow and William Bales, each contributing new aspects, until the modern dance as it began is scarcely seen any more; in its place is a sort of theater dance with a dramatic modern accent. Examples of this newer form are found in such dance dramas as Doris Humphrey's *Day on Earth*, Martha Graham's *Letter to the World*, and José Limon's *The Moor's Pavane*, the last-named using the handkerchief motif of Shakespeare's *Othello*. Evolving, then, from the dance as emotional expression and pictorial movement, modern dance has come all the way from the ritualistic movements of worship and folk dances to the highly specialized form of dance drama that is sometimes presented not only with music and scenery but even with the use of the voice as well, in song or dialogue, as for instance in Nina Fonaroff's *Mr. Puppet*, or Charles Weidman's *On My Mother's Side* and its sequel, *And Daddy Was a Fireman*.

Today the choreographer tends to build his dance drama as the playwright builds his play, with an eye to making clear to his audience the psychological motivations of his characters.

The DRAME is a stirring play of serious theme, presenting characters in an arresting situation and developing a strong plot by emotional expectancy. The term is seldom used except academically, but we approximate the French word "drame" in our popular use of the expression "a drama" when we use that term casually to designate a thoughtful, full-emotioned play. This type is said to stand on its "big scene," because it always builds in crescendo toward a thrilling climax, and every part is played for the fortissimo effect. To name such plays is to recall such scenes, pregnant with the quality of "theater": Walter's *Paid in Full*, Bernstein's *The Thief*, Klein's *The Lion and the Mouse*, Fitch's *The Truth*, Brieux's *The Red Robe*, even perhaps Hellman's *The Little Foxes*.

The EXTRAVAGANZA is a musical burlesque designed to produce its effect by humorous irregularity, overstatement, overdrawing of caricature, and overlauding of sentiment. In the last quarter of the nineteenth century the extravaganza undermined the French *opéra bouffe*. In the hands of W. S. Gilbert and Arthur Sullivan it became a timely commentary on events of the day with an audacious impudence in characterization and a rollicking hodgepodge of tunes. There have been other composers of that particular form of musical play, but the best-known extravaganzas remain *H.M.S. Pinafore*, *The Mikado*, *The Pirates of Penzance*, and the other Gilbert-Sullivan hits of a former generation.

The FANTASY is a theatrical representation of the chimerical; at its best, poetic; at its worst, sentimentalized. A whole play, such as Yeat's *The Land of Heart's Desire*, may be done in the spirit of fantasy, but it is more common to find the element of fantasy coloring a play which is rooted, if not nourished, in reality. This element of fantasy is prominent in many of the plays of James M. Barrie, as for instance the dream scene in *A Kiss for Cinderella*. The Xanadu interlude in Connelly and Kaufman's *Beggar on Horse-*

back is fantasy with a satirical edge; and there is certainly fantasy in any Saroyan play, even in one as seemingly realistic as *The Time of Your Life.*

The INTERLUDE is a light dramatic entertainment introduced between acts of a longer play. It may have the character of farce, fantasy, or comedy. The old mystery and morality plays made use of the interlude, introducing through it a feature in celebration of some particular fete.

LITURGICAL DRAMA is the drama of worship. The Greeks made use of it in certain public festivals, and later the Romans used it in the development of the celebration of Communion. The Reformation put a quietus on liturgical drama in some localities but a present-day tendency is reviving the form, enriched by the free use of poetry, an elaboration of interpretative musical participation, and even by the interpretative dance.

The MASQUE is a short, allegorical play in which the characters represent symbolical or mythical personalities. It is a figurative story suggesting an idea not expressly stated, and clings in form to the derivation of the word "allegory," describing one thing under the image of another.

The masque was used by the Greeks to reflect satirically certain human foibles which were brought to the fore by a particular civic or political situation. Sometimes the masque became a parable depicting a fictitious narrative under the guise of facts familiar to the audience. During the sixteenth and seventeenth centuries Italian drama elaborated the masque with dancing, dumb show, and the use of stock characters into an improvised comedy of wide popularity. Pantalone, Pullicinella, and Harlequin were among the stereotyped characters who operated in a variety of amusing situations. Harlequin, usually the servant of Pantalone and the lover of Columbina, inherited his sword and his drolleries from the character of the devil as played in the more riotous mystery plays. *Pilgrim's Progress,* when presented upon a stage, becomes a masque, although of greater length than the typical masque. For modern presentation the masque closely skirts the pageant.

The MIRACLE PLAYS, the MORALITIES, and the MYSTERIES all grew out of church presentations.

The MYSTERIES were the dramatic presentation of Scriptural events, particularly the central mystery of the redemption of the world as accomplished by the Nativity, the Passion, and the Resurrection. Fairly early in the history of the church, certain of the clergy, to make the Mass more vivid and relate it to the experience of the people, began to act out the great moments of their religion. So the mysteries came into being.

The mystery did not follow chronological order in the presentation of events. The shepherds, on their way to worship the Child at Bethlehem, might sing of the deeper mysteries of the Eucharist. The hermit who sometimes accompanied the shepherds might tell his beads and address time and space. Since Christmas and Easter were intrinsically dramatic festivals, their stories were easily elaborated into plays. St. Francis, among others, combining his gift of imagination with a simple realism, presented the Christmas story to his friends of Assisi with a real manger, a living baby, and all the barnyard animals. Only the star, hung upon a wire, was artificial. The Wakefield Mysteries, thirty-two in number, frequently referred to as the Towneley Cycle, were among the most popular. They are considered superior in vivacity and humor, and point toward the freer movement of the moralities. The mysteries were not presented as esoteric philosophy hidden from the uninitiated, but as the simple revelation of holy things. The mechanical devices and stage tricks frequently made of the mystery almost a miraculous spectacle with colorful flying angels, fire-spitting dragons, and animals of tremendous size which emitted strange cries and made threatening advances. No miracle seems to have been too marvelous to frustrate reproduction except, perhaps, Jonah and the whale.

As the artificial tricks of the stage became more complicated, their stories put out ramifications. The miracle plays put in their appearance.

MIRACLE PLAYS were based on the legends of the saints. Few playwrights stand out as individuals. Hroswitha, a German nun of the tenth century, modeled her presentations after Terence, except that chastity in all her plays was the great virtue. St. Hilary, a pupil of Abelard, left three Latin plays of some dramatic movement. Many of the French miracle plays were very long (one of them with forty thousand lines, something over four times the length of the Shakespearean tragedies) and were really a series of running scenes rather than a story moving toward a climax.

Certain formalities of production came to be recognized: divine personages were shown with gilt hair and beards, Herod was portrayed as a Saracen, souls wore black or white coats according to their spiritual counterparts, angels had gold skins and wings. Finally the miracle plays made their way into the vernacular, broadened their scope, and lost their identity as legends of the saints. Some of the legends of the miracles, however, such as that of *The Juggler of Notre Dame*, have made a permanent place for themselves in later drama.

MORALITIES were plays whose characters personified certain virtues or qualities and allegorically illustrated some truth. They were a link between the strictly religious drama and the secular drama. The mysteries were largely associated with church services. The miracle plays became guild productions, given by lay associations in honor of their own patron saint in their own guildhall. But the early moralities, in the time of Henry VI and Henry VII, used any story which might allegorize the conflict between good and evil. Probably the best-known morality play is *Everyman*. During the Elizabethan age the moralities not only carried a weight of theological teaching but became media for preaching morality.

The increased use of the comic element marked the development of the moralities as popular plays. The devil was accompanied by his vice, in a fool's habit, reflecting the custom of the court fool. The vice made it his part to tease the devil for the edification and amusement of the audience. Nor was one devil sufficient. The antics of a whole corps of devils competed for approval, and sometimes the virtues became only a background against which the devils raised havoc. In such fashion the moralities rioted their way into secular drama and forgot, for a time, the motives that had inspired them.

The MUSICAL COMEDY is obviously a play which carries its story by spoken dialogue interspersed with songs. It had its rise in the English ballad opera, which came as a protest against the stolid, formal Italian opera of the early eighteenth century. The continued use of recitative gave place to the spoken dialogue of the musical comedy. Gay's *The Beggar's Opera* defined the musical comedy as a separate dramatic form destined to fill a place of its own in the modern theater.

Until recent years musical comedy tended toward a stereotype of the sentiments and stock characters of an older melodrama, with the addition of gorgeous spectacle and vaudeville acts, and had the flavor of sentimental comedy. Later musical comedies, however, such as *Of Thee I Sing* and *Lady in the Dark* are brightened by satire, and musicals such as *Oklahoma* and *Brigadoon* have a folklore quality that differentiates them from the older type. The best of musicals today have kept pace with, if they have not outstripped, other plays in depicting folkways and posing current problems. Hammerstein and Rodgers, in taking over Lynn Riggs's play *Green Grow the Lilacs*, deleting most of the melodrama and adding the timely lyrics as well as Miss De Mille's choreography, probably realized in *Oklahoma* the picture of American folkways that Riggs himself may have hoped for in the original play. *Finian's Rainbow* posed a problem of racial equality which would have been taboo in the musical of an older day; and certainly *South Pacific* is far more than a romantic story.

MUSIC DRAMA. A new type of musical play, or play through music, has come on to the stage with a bow to its parents, the dramatic play and the opera. Since the opera was itself a hybrid form, it would seem that any play of high dramatic quality in which the lines are sung instead of spoken would still be opera. And maybe the music drama is opera by definition, but if so it is a new kind

of opera in which lines never appear to be sung only to display vocal
pyrotechnics but always as genuine expressions of character and
story. *Four Saints in Three Acts*, in which Gertrude Stein and
Virgil Thompson collaborated, was a move toward the new form,
although customarily spoken of as modern opera. Then Menotti,
in his comedies *The Telephone* and *The Old Maid and the Thief*
and in his short tragedy *The Medium* presented a more closely
unified integration of drama and music in which the dialogue is
sung but not reiterated for the sake of musical effects. In *The
Consul*, Menotti uses such ordinary characters as might be found
almost any day in almost any consul's office, gives them the desperation of necessary escape from some Gestapo threat, and lets the
story grow from character caught in circumstance; certainly the
materials of modern tragedy. His music also seems to grow from
character, as if it were the necessary expression of the character's
predicament and personality, and so the total impression upon an
audience is that of a highly dramatic play with emotional overtones
effected through the music. Other dramatists than Menotti appear
to be experimenting with modifications of this compact but fluid
dramatic form, which in its integration of music and drama somewhat resembles modern ballet as distinguished from the earlier
ballet wherein technique and pictorial effect had precedence over
all else.

An OPERA is an elaborate drama set to music. Naturally the plot
selected for opera is especially adaptable to musical accompaniment
and rich in emotional appeal in order to sustain the convention of
singing rather than speaking the dialogue. Opera seems particularly
to demand costumes, scenery, and action.

The composers of opera may be said to take the same liberty with
time as a dimension of reality that certain modern painters take
with the space dimension of reality. Just as El Greco and many of
his followers elongate the lines of the figure to make a pattern
emphasizing their interpretation of reality, so composers of opera
elongate certain intervals of time to encompass their full emotional

content, in order to make more real the actual quality of those moments. Thus, at certain tension points, we have an aria occupying several minutes to express an idea which might be put into a few short sentences. This ignoring of the actualities of time in the interest of a specialized emotional appeal is, perhaps, the only original contribution opera has made to the field of drama.

Opera began in the last part of the sixteenth century with a Florentine revival of the Greek use of musical declamation. Among the revivalists was Vincenzo Galilei, the father not only of opera but of the Galileo who made a science of astronomy. Neither Galilei nor his friends had any idea what the Greek musical accompaniments had been, but they saw freedom in the very absence of such knowledge. Before that time music had been used in drama, indeed within drama, for the masque and pastorals were frequently enlivened with melody. But music as an accompaniment to the spoken line, which gradually forsook the recitative and became an exercise in vocalization, was new. Frequently the librettos of the great operas are derived from distinguished plays like *Faust* and *Pelleas and Melisande*. So, on at least one side of the family, the art has an accepted parent.

In the presentation of opera the musical prelude is a common device to set the audience thinking in a musical way. Solos and multiplied combinations of voices, including the full chorus, carry the main body of the story. The narrative elements are given in recitative, which bridges the emotional high points more easily than a lapse into the spoken word. Opera composers of our own day tend to be purists in their resentment of arias for show. Since the advent of Richard Wagner opera has been much more really a music drama. However, in opera the enrichment of thought and emotion by the use of music is counterbalanced by a loss of naturalness and a slowing of action which the music makes necessary.

OPÉRA BOUFFE is French comic opera, marked by buffoonery and burlesque, constructed on too light a scale to be ranked as *opéra comique*. OPERA BUFFA is the Italian opera of light, playful character built around a comic subject—frequently, indeed, an extravagantly comic subject.

OPÉRA COMIQUE is French comic opera, essentially the same as *opera buffa* except that the dialogue is spoken instead of being sung.

OPERETTA is, literally, a little opera and technically is confined to a one-act production, such as Rossini's *L'inganno felice* and Mozart's *Schauspieldirektor*. But in English the term is used to describe almost any light or comic opera. It is applied particularly, although loosely, to a musical-dramatic work not too difficult to perform, a composite of gay music, amusing plot, and clever and sentimental lines.

An ORATORIO is a religious text set to music for solo voices, choruses, and instruments, and is always presented without action, costumes, or scenery. For some time the oratorio has been separable from the liturgy although its source may have been in the incidental music of the miracle plays, which in turn were an enrichment of the liturgy. Perhaps the earliest form was the recitation of the Passion story during Holy Week by the early church. In this recitation the words of the evangel were sung in Gregorian tones by the tenor, with other voices carrying the direct discourse of other participants. Most modern oratorios follow the pattern of Handel, Mozart, Beethoven, in using Scriptural theme for the dramatic text and an orchestral accompaniment for the vocal music of recitative, arias, and choruses.

A PAGEANT is an elaborate pictorial presentation of narrative designed to give a unified total impression. In the pageant the use of dialogue is optional, and less important than the color and movement of the presentation. There is no stereotyped technique for its structure. It may be large, loose, and sprawling or a simple, compact succession of realistic scenes. Each episode is complete in itself but partakes of the total unity and builds toward a climax. At the present time pageants generally fall into two classes: historical pageants, presenting the life of a community, and idealizational pageants, presenting religious, social, or civic standards. The historical pageant may show the growth of a small community or the development of multiplied cultures. It may be planned to honor a specific event or a particular person. Idealizational pageants may personify, allegorize, and symbolize. The pageant uses numerous accessories: chorus, band, orchestra, dance, poetry, tableau, and stately, showy spectacle effects. It is presented in various settings both out of doors and indoors, on a stage or within an arena— almost any place where there is room for processions, elaborate parade, and pictorial grouping of figures.

The term "pageant" is also sometimes used to refer to the plays that were presented on what the English called "pageants"— movable stages on wheels, the sort of thing we call a float today. These could be taken from one part of town to another, a separate play being given on each stage and a separate audience waiting at each station. The mystery and miracle cycles were presented on such wagons (frequently two-deck carriages) or on a movable scaffolding, which permitted an all-day performance of loosely woven stories such as the entire Bible narrative. But the pageant plays, despite the fact that their performance assured a holiday from business, also paled. They were heavy, they were coarse, and—more fatal to a play—they were childishly lacking in that combination of movement, imagination, and suspense which makes theater.

A PANTOMIME is a play without words, a play of movements and attitudes, as the derivation of its name would show—pantos, "all," plus mimos, "mimic," "mime." Some early pantomimes, such as those of the Romans, were performed by masked actors, the mimicry being wholly body movements, but later development allowed the addition of facial expression and thereby enriched the mimicry.

Because pantomime is literally a dumb show in which the actors have no recourse to words to help convey their meaning, it is usually necessary to use a story known to the audience. The other ancient alternative to using a well-known tale was to interpolate a chorus which sang the story being acted. The early Greeks, Chinese, and Indians used this method of re-enacting hero myths with which the audience was already familiar. In Italy pantomime developed the characters of Harlequin, Pantalone, Columbina, and Scaramouch. The mimic plays of other European countries and of America have borrowed these stock characters. The two extremes of pantomime are most popular in modern use: the sprightly pantomime-buffoonery of the burlesque and the stately, dignified pantomime-picture relevant to the Christmas celebration.

The REVUE is a melange of songs, sketches, ballets and other dances, and sometimes spectacles, bound together chiefly by a topical interest. At its best the revue is a satirical commentary on events of the day and on human foibles in general. It is to the drama what the cartoon is to the newspaper—or the cartoon plus the "columns" and the rotogravure section. Such a revue is smart, alertly of today, but often under the label of "revue" we are given a happy-go-lucky spectacle, its pattern more akin to vaudeville than to that of the true revue of topical, satirical intent.

The SATIRE is a dramatic production which calls attention to social conditions by holding them up to rebuke through ridicule. The satire dares a severity of remark and a caustic, trenchant wit.

The comedies of Aristophanes are representative of the use of satire as a measure of reform. Nothing in Athens was sacred to his vigorous comic genius. He took his fling at all things political, at all personages whom the populace took too seriously (or who took themselves too seriously), at the status quo and each of the pillars that supported it, but especially at vice, cowardice, and deceit. A different sort of satirist was Molière. The designs for his plays came from everywhere. He borrowed plots from Spain, situations from Italy, and anything he could use from the classicists. But he used them only to express character, and usually the expression was lightly, laughably, but genuinely satirical. Contemporary society furnished his models; nobles, peasants, priests, doctors, politicians, writers, actors, and all the rest came within the compass of his wit.

With a satire that was sometimes whimsical, sometimes generous, but usually sympathetic, he made his characters laugh at one another and the audience at all of them.

Satire demands a certain urbanity impossible for the too-earnest. Only the playwright who combines social understanding, an ability to use sarcasm deftly, and a keen sense of the ridiculous can handle satire effectively. With Bernard Shaw, in a play like *Arms and the Man*, satire becomes a sort of social lash whose cutting provides something like a stinging enjoyment; and Giraudoux in *The Mad Woman of Chaillot* reaches through current acceptance of social values to the basic disparities upon which they rest, throwing the world askew so that a madwoman appears more sane than the sane and thereby offers a shadow line of balance against which the audience while it laughs can at least glimpse the fact of its own off-centeredness. With Barrie, in such a play as *The Admirable Crichton*, the satire is pleasant while penetrating. Tarkington and Wilson, in *The Man from Home*, managed to laugh both with and at their fellow countrymen so sympathetically that the satirical intent was lost in the sentimental content. But whatever the mood the playwright may choose, satire tends to point an overbearing vice or virtue by making it ridiculous.

The STATIC PLAY is the one in which characters and situation are the same at the end of the play as in the beginning. Both characters and circumstances are held in place by forces acting upon them. Instead of being driven toward a goal, the characters are prevented from reaching a goal. The word "static" is true to its original meaning of "acting by mere weight without motion." Such a play is Chekhov's *The Cherry Orchard*, and therefore obviously Joshua Logan's *The Wisteria Trees*, which is a transplanting of the Chekhov characters and situations to Louisiana at the turn of the century. At best, the characters make only the semblance of a struggle, and are really passive against the changing conditions of the old order becoming the new. They remain in a state of equilibrium, held there by the very forces they wish to be freed from.

A SKIT is a short dramatic episode usually satirical or humorous. It is a sketch drawn in few lines, suggesting the story that a larger canvas might depict. The skit finds its place in the bill of vaudeville, revue, burlesque, or any of the loosely built dramatic forms. Some of the better skits of recent times have been those written by Noel Coward and acted by Beatrice Lillie.

A TABLEAU is a vivid representation of a picture by a group of persons who remain motionless in appropriate postures, sometimes interpreted by an interlocutor but not necessitating speech on the part of the actors. The materials for tableaus are as multiple as ordinary human interests: "Charles Dickens' Child-Characters," "Priscilla and John Alden," the Signing of the Declaration of Independence, and in almost every town and hamlet at Christmas, the Nativity. Any situation or scene which lends itself to pictorial still-life representation may become a tableau.

Frequently the nineteenth-century playwright was not satisfied to let the curtain stay down at the close of an act, but had it lifted immediately to discover the actors grouped in a tableau to epitomize the action just accomplished; and so in some old plays reprinted today one may still find the terse stage direction "Tableau" at the termination of each act.

VAUDEVILLE is a variety show composed of separate acts, loosely threaded together on a string of lively tunes. The acts may be musical, dramatic, acrobatic, low comedy, tableau, or partake of almost any conceivable character providing they are short and timed to meet the immediate interest of the audience.

Vaudeville draws its name from a small village in Normandy famed for the composition of lively, piquant songs composed of couplets and refrain and carrying a topical interest. This topical interest is no longer necessary to the vaudeville act, the emphasis of the bill having shifted to variety, spectacular effect, and personal appearances from radio and cinema.

PART TWO

❦

The Play Itself: Structure and Technique

Essentials of the Play

NATURALLY, all plays—tragedy, comedy, farce, and melodrama—have certain essentials in common. They all deal with character, situation, theme, and mood. Indeed, we have said pages ago, and rather boldly, that these essentials can even be made into a formula to define the play. And yet, as in all art, the sum of the parts does not equal the whole.

This is one of the discoveries that almost everyone makes, sooner or later, for himself. If he is an analyzer, he analyzes the thing that is made and sees exactly how the parts fit together, but when he throws his analysis into reverse and tries to synthesize the whole he discovers that no number of rules can teach a man to create unless he has the creative spirit to begin with. If, on the other hand, he is himself creative he discovers that his creating begins where the rules leave off. Indeed, he is probably unconscious of the rules. And if his attention is called to them, either because of his excellence in fulfilling them or his temerity in ignoring them, he is likely to be rather startled. For he did not set out either to fulfill or to ignore. He was merely making. Plainly, following all the rules does not make a play.

But fortunately creating a play is not man's only function. The man who analyzes has a particular satisfaction of his own. In point of time the analyzer comes after the creative writer. The Aristotelian "laws" of the drama came after Aeschylus, Sophocles, Euripides, and Aristophanes. Undoubtedly, in the beginning someone made something and an onlooker wondered how he had made that thing. When the inlooker figured out what he considered to be the maker's process he called it the law-of-making-that-thing. But they never quite got together, the maker of the thing and the maker of the rules, for as often as not the maker of the thing really hadn't made it that way and more often than not the maker of the rules didn't care to create at all.

In each generation the makers go on making and the explainers go on explaining and every century or so some creator smashes the old rules and some explainer has to build new rules and start again. All in all, probably the analyzer understands the creator a bit better than the creator understands the analyzer. For it is always difficult for the creator to believe that the exactness of a rule can possibly describe that thing which grew so spontaneously, or so rebelliously, within him. When James M. Barrie was asked to write an introduction to a volume by a fellow playwright, he "cautiously"—so he says—bought a book on playwriting in order to see if the other man had written his plays "properly." But Barrie hastens to add that "the book was so learned, and the author knew so much, and the subject when studied grew so difficult" that he hurriedly abandoned his inquiry. "Thus one of us at least missed his last chance of discovering what that mysterious thing, 'stage technique,' really is." One may take the implications of such a pleasantry at less or more than face value, but at any rate no one seems to know better than the writer of plays that rules do not make a playwright or mold his plays.

Occasionally, however, even a playwright wishes to know the technicalities, and indeed there are some playwrights who believe that a knowledge of the parts facilitates their craftsmanship. Be that as it may, from whatever angle we approach the play we come to the essentials—character, situation, theme, and mood. These essentials may stand as a sort of line drawing of dramaturgics, pointing those elements without which there can be no play. But even with a diagram at hand it is impossible to say arbitrarily where to begin the study of a play. Does theme come first? Or situation? Or character? Or mood? Which came first to the playwright's mind? Who can say? About all that we can safely say is that no matter how the playwright approaches his play he cannot get far before he is dealing with characters, for if drama is a doing—and it is never anything else—then the doing is by someone, and as soon as we think of the doing in terms of the doer we are beginning to think of character.

CHARACTER. We are familiar enough in daily life with the actions that spring from character. Suddenly, on a day which might otherwise have been ordinary, news explodes that someone has discovered the slim microbe that causes the great white plague. Telegraph and cable wires ask, "Who did this thing?" And then reporters dig out the story of an unpretentious doctor, with nearsighted eyes, thin hands blackened from bichloride of mercury, who has always been a fiend for experimentation. From fact to theory he has made his stubborn way, from theory to a hundred more facts, a thousand facts, then demonstrations which turn question marks to periods and begin new paragraphs in human history. Nothing that Robert Koch did was so amazing as himself, working without precedent and creating the very rules he worked by. His "story," modified though it may have been by environment and even by chance, grew out of his character in a real and practical sense. He himself motivated the event that made the headline.

And so, quite simply in the drama all about us, in our family, in our friends, in our celebrities, we are interested in some persons more than in others. For reasons which may be simple or profound, with some we have a common denominator of interests. We identify their ambitions, desires, defeats, burdens, accomplishments with our own, and have a personal stake in their well-being. They have for some reason captured our attention and so we follow them through what they do, and presently we see that what they do grows out of what they are; the things they do are the things they must do, being the sort of persons they are. When we find ourselves so following the stories of characters in a play we may be sure that they are the stories of tragedy and comedy, for tragedies and comedies are primarily plays about persons rather than plays about situations.

SITUATION. Sometimes, when we see persons caught in a set of

circumstances about which they must do something, we are intrigued by their situation. We are more interested in the doing than
in the doer; that is, some happenings are in themselves amusing or
interesting or hair raising. The average person laughs when he sees
a fat man falling, and does not stop to ask who has slipped nor to
analyze why he thinks the fall is funny. Also the average person is
excited when he hears that a stranger in the apartment next door
has been robbed and gagged and might have been killed if the
detectives had not arrived in the nick of time. And why did the
detectives arrive? Well, that is the story. It grows out of the situation, and the identity of the stranger is relatively unimportant. These
stories from situations are, when put upon the stage, the stories of
farce and of melodrama.

THEME. But plays are more than characters and situation. The
playwright has a thought about the characters and the destiny they
develop from their situation. This thought is his theme. His theme,
however, is not always mapped out in his mind in the same way
that a road is mapped out leading to an end which the builder
foresees. Sometimes, indeed, the playwright is almost unconscious
that he is moving toward a given destination—that he has a thought
directed toward an end—for while a play is being written characters frequently seem to have an independence which makes the
author feel almost incidental to the play. Then eventually he discovers—or someone tells him!—what his theme is and he sees that
he has had a theme all the time. For with the play already written it
is comparatively easy, as it is when reviewing one's own life, to look
back and see how a given situation was really conditioned by a
preceding situation and before that by a still earlier series of situations until eventually all have run together in a theme. Thus situations are not strung on a theme like beads on a cord, they are woven
into the fabric of the play like figures in a tapestry and, as in the
tapestry, the motif or theme becomes apparent when the pattern
is finished.

MOOD. But even theme and character and situation are not all.

Sometimes the playwright is not at first conscious of character or situation or theme, and his play comes upon him mood-first. In that case he may suddenly find himself in a happily irritable state. He is emotionally at white heat, although about what he is not quite sure. Yet at any moment he will come through with characters that walk and talk and go places. To describe a playwright in this state when his play is coming upon him mood-first is to make him sound a little daft, but probably he would be the first indifferently to admit the adjective.

Of course, a playwright may have as many moods as he has plays, but each play, if he is wise, has only one mood. Again, it is plain that mood, like theme, is not a thing separate from the rest of the play. The very fact that some prefer to call this essential of the play atmosphere instead of mood indicates at once its illusive but permeating quality. It is the tone of the play, the temper, the volatile essence. It cannot be thrown over the characters like a cloak nor in any other way handled as a thing apart; it permeates the whole play somewhat as chlorophyll permeates a blade of grass, it is as obvious as chlorophyll and as resistant to complete explanation.

However, to translate a mood into action, into drama, the playwright necessarily uses characters in a situation, propelled by a thought, and so we are back at our formula. But whether a formula is more helpful when we stick to it or when we depart from it will have to be determined by those who know whether a fence around a field is more useful for keeping cows in or for keeping them out. We purpose now gathering together those elements in a play which appear to belong in the field of characterization, leaving the gates open.

Character

IN THE presentation of his characters, there are a number of ways in which a playwright may make them known to us in the limited time at his disposal. He may do it by means of setting, by means of mere physical action, by personal appearance, by out-and-out description, and—most surely—by the action that is more than physical.

By setting. Because he has to catch our interest almost instantly, the playwright seldom overlooks the device of making his stage setting tell something, and frequently the stage setting is his first device of characterization. Through the setting he tells us even before we see the characters what sort of persons they are likely to be.

When the curtains rise on Maugham's *The Circle* we see "a stately drawing room . . . with fine pictures on the walls and Georgian furniture. . . . It is not a house but a place." And so we expect to see sophisticated persons, not the nondescript characters of Rice's *Street Scene.* As soon as Arnold Champion-Cheney comes in, rings for the butler, alters the position of one of the chairs, and blows dust from an ornament on the chimneypiece, we surmise that this is the person characterized by the setting. We knew him, somewhat, before he appeared.

By physical action. Mr. Maugham now proceeds at once to use one of the commonest and most effective methods of characterization, that of characterizing by physical action. Arnold rearranges the chair, he blows dust from the ornament, in brief, while he is searching for his wife his eye is on his furniture and its arrangement. He is *that* sort of man. But when Teddie Luton comes on a little later we know almost as quickly through that young man's actions that

he would scarcely ever have his eye on the furniture—any furniture
—and certainly not while searching for Elizabeth.

By *personal appearance.* Naturally the playwright does not over-
look characterization by personal appearance. Arnold is "tall and
good-looking. . . . He has a look that is intellectual but somewhat
bloodless." Teddie is "an attractive youth in flannels." This method
of characterization by personal appearance is altogether too obvious
to elaborate, and if a playwright depended upon such a bald attempt at characterizing he would probably be an unproduced, and
unread, playwright.

By *what others say.* Characters are also, of course, unavoidably
characterized by what other characters say about them. Like the
method of characterization through personal appearance, this
method is too patent to need elaboration. But frequently the way in
which a character describes another character also describes the person making the observation and so the playwright serves a double
purpose with his dialogue. For instance, when Arnold says before
Teddie appears, "I don't know that he's very intelligent, but, you
know, there are occasions when you *want* a bull in a china shop,"
we get something of the flavor of Arnold's temperament as well as
preparation for the entrance of Teddie.

Sometimes, too, when a character is mistaken in describing an
individual who has not yet appeared, the individual's entrance is
heightened. Either we are caught up in quick surprise, having expected a different sort of person, or we are pleasantly complacent,
saying to ourselves, "Well, I thought so all the time." Thus Elizabeth's description of what she thinks Lady Kitty may be like is all
the more effective because Elizabeth is mistaken. Even while we
are listening to her we feel that somehow she cannot be right. In
her own mind Elizabeth has built up a picture of the mother whom
even Arnold cannot remember, because the errant Lady Kitty ran
away with Lord Porteous when Arnold was only five. Elizabeth is
romantically impressed by the fact that Lady Kitty gave up her

home, her position, and her child for the sake of the man she loved. Now for the first time, after thirty years, Lady Kitty and Lord Porteous are coming back on a visit at the invitation of Elizabeth. "I seem to know her already," says Elizabeth in anticipation. "I think her face is a little sad, for a love like that doesn't leave you gay, it leaves you grave, but I think her pale face is unlined. It's like a child's . . . I imagine her slight and frail. . . . With beautiful thin hands and white hair. I've pictured her so often in that Renaissance palace they live in, with old masters on the walls and lovely carved things all around, sitting in a black silk dress with old lace round her neck and old-fashioned diamonds. . . ."

And then Lady Kitty arrives. The butler announces: "Lady Catherine Champion-Cheney. Lord Porteous." They enter, and Elizabeth sees her for the first time, "a gay little lady, with dyed hair and painted cheeks. She is somewhat outrageously dressed. She never forgets that she has been a pretty woman and she still behaves as if she were twenty-five." Moments like this give us the "expected unexpected" that is one of the legitimate thrills of the theater. Even before her entrance we know a good deal about Lady Kitty. Upon first sight of her we know a lot more. We begin to understand her. And she merely sums up our understanding when in the third act we hear her say, "It's no joke when you have to rely on yourself to keep a man. I could never afford to grow old. . . . However tired I've been I've had to be brilliant and gay." It was all there implicitly in her first appearance, and Elizabeth's mistaken description served only to italicize the characterization—as well as to give us an insight into the character of Elizabeth herself.

By what they say about themselves. Of course, much of our information about characters comes from what they themselves say, from what they tell us about themselves and others. Even their manner of speaking frequently discloses traits of character. Arnold speaks with precision and we could guess that he would correct Elizabeth, good-naturedly, for saying "damn" instead of "oh, bother." We further expect him to take the position that he will stand by anything that he has said. He looks and acts and speaks like one who would.

When Teddie comes in a few minutes later, his opening lines are equally characteristic:

TEDDIE. I say, what about this tennis?
ELIZABETH. Come in. We're having a scene.
TEDDIE. How splendid! What about?
ELIZABETH. The English language.
TEDDIE. Don't tell me you've been splitting your infinitives.

And there, in his words and in his manner of speaking, is Teddie, who knows what things in life are important and takes all the others lightly.

Lord Porteous's first speech is "Ugh!" and his second is: "Damnable roads you've got down here. How d'you do, my dear? Why d'you have such damnable roads in England?" It isn't, of course, the roads that matter to the audience. It is the fact that Lord Porteous is gruff and disgruntled, and perhaps unhappy at heart. Lady Kitty's first speech is: "Elizabeth! Elizabeth! What an adorable creature! Hughie, isn't she adorable!" Lady Kitty whose effusive words say so little and disclose so much.

Elizabeth tells us a great deal about herself directly when she says to Lady Kitty: "I'm not suited for this sort of existence. Arnold wants me to take what he calls my place in society. Oh, I get so bored with those parties in London. All those middle-aged painted women, in beautiful clothes, lolloping around ballrooms with rather old young men. And the endless luncheons where they gossip about So-and-so's love affairs."

Teddie tells us even more about himself—and about Elizabeth as he understands her—when he answers her remark that in deciding to stay with Arnold she is giving up all hope of happiness. "But I wasn't offering you happiness," he says. "I don't think my sort of love tends to happiness. I'm jealous. I'm not an easy man to get on with. I'm often out of temper and irritable. I should be fed to the teeth with you sometimes, and so would you be with me. I dare say we'd fight like cat and dog, and sometimes we'd hate each other. Often you'd be wretched and bored stiff and lonely, and often you'd be frightfully homesick, and then you'd regret all you'd lost. Stupid women would be rude to you because we'd run away together. And some of them would cut you. I don't offer you peace and happiness. I offer you unrest and anxiety. I don't offer you happiness. I offer you love."

By action. But the basic method of disclosing character is always through action. Action, it must be understood, embraces far more than physical movement. Mere physical action is sometimes little more than mannerism, it is often incidental. Real action springs from the deep wells of purpose, of will, of character. There is, for instance, the action of Teddie Luton in carrying off Elizabeth. The physical action is obvious. He wraps a cloak about her, they drive off into the night in Lord Porteous's automobile. But the real action is the taking of her, taking her away from her husband, away from her accustomed life to his own harder, simpler life in the Federated Malay States, to a life which he has warned her does not hold "happiness." Arnold's offer to open a bank account in Elizabeth's name so that she may not be in need of anything also is action that springs from character. He means to hold her to him by his generosity, and the act of presenting himself as a magnanimous husband ready to divide his fortune and to sacrifice his political career discloses the real Arnold, who cannot bear to have a wife or a piece of furniture out of place.

But more fundamental to the play than Teddie's action or Arnold's is the action that goes on inside of Elizabeth's mind. Her going away, which we literally see before our eyes, is the less significant part of her action. Indeed, it is merely an objectification of the psychological action that has brought her through crisis to decision and finally results in her leaving. For Teddie does not take her. She goes. As Lady Kitty went. Of all the main characters in the play, Elizabeth—who does the least physically—travels the longest road. And yet even Elizabeth's action is not the play. Deeper still is the reaction of generation to generation—Kitty, Porteous, and Champion-Cheney on the one side, Elizabeth, Teddie Luton, and Arnold on the other—which is common to the recurring pattern of life and makes of it the circle symbolized in the title.

MOTIVATION. All these methods of characterization are more or less objective. They are ways of letting us see and hear the character. But actually it is something behind actions and words which convinces us of a character's reality. We need to know why he acts as he does, we need to know his motivation. For motivation is the inner compulsion that determines choice and impels action, and an individual's actions are seen in their full significance only when we know his motivation. His doings and sayings are only vents in his mask through which we see his actual countenance and there read this why of things.

Although we see the people about us in terms of situation, we understand them in terms of motivation. Their actions are comparatively meaningless except as we are able to sense what they want of life and why they want it. Perhaps we say of someone, "I don't understand what makes him act like that." And then one day something gives us a clue to his ambition, his prejudice, his affection, or some other impulsion, and we say, "Now I understand him!" His motivation has made his actions meaningful.

In life we can afford to wait—indeed, we usually have to wait—for motivation to manifest itself. But in a play, where everything is necessarily foreshortened, it is essential that something of the motivation of a character be made clear rather soon after he is presented to us. So we have the references to previous events, the disclosure of a character's antecedents, or any other thrust into the inner nature of a character which will disclose why he does what he does, why he thinks as he thinks, and "how he got that way." And since whenever possible it is the playwright's aim to show instead of tell, he presents motivating action early in the play; he lets us hear the Weird Sisters tempt Macbeth, he lets us see Krogstad confront Nora, he lets us watch Chris reading Anna's letter, he lets us listen as François Villon boasts in the presence of the disguised Louis XI, he lets us hear Roxane confide to Cyrano her love for Christian.

In our social intercourse we are automatically selective, at least half the remarks our acquaintances make and half the actions they perform before our eyes are scarcely heard and seen by us. The things we retain are largely those which disclose motivation, or which lead us to wonder about motivation. Upon the stage, where time and interest are far more at a premium, the playwright consciously makes that same selection for us. Even the things that seem inconsequential are usually motivated and thus give clarity to characterization and compactness to structure. In the procedure of the law courts, the first thing that a prosecutor in a criminal case must establish is a motive for the crime. Unless he establishes a motive, and establishes that motive "beyond a reasonable doubt," his case is weak if not lost from the start. The procedure of the theater is much the same. If the playwright does not make clear the motives that impel his characters to action, his case too is lost.

Motivation is the key to action. If Lonsdale in *The Last of Mrs. Cheyney* had given us no hint as to the sort of person his central character was—that is, if he had not motivated Mrs. Cheyney's actions—we would have been baffled when she prepared to steal the necklace. We might have felt that she was just another professional crook. Or, worse, we might have imagined that she had a large number of dependents to feed and no other way than stealing to acquire the wherewithal. The very idea sounds farfetched but that is because Lonsdale did take care to let us surmise ahead of time that this might be Mrs. Cheyney's first attempt and that her gang, posing as her servants, expected her to get that necklace to prove her cleverness. In *What Every Woman Knows* Barrie motivates John Shand's housebreaking so that we are willing to accept this breach of convention although most of us do not ordinarily condone housebreaking. The motivation explains John Shand and through it we understand his acts. It gives him verisimilitude even though we have never actually known a man who broke into libraries in order to study. But we feel that we know John Shand because we have experienced—actually or imaginatively—the same motivation that makes him act as he does.

PLAUSIBILITY. It is motivation that helps to make a play plausible. The audience, especially in this day, demands that a deed be plausible, and the playwright knows that it is almost impossible to make an action seem plausible unless it is motivated through character.

Before the term "psychology" found its way into popularity Shakespeare made use of the commonplace fact that a deed appears plausible only when it seems the natural thing for a given character to do under the circumstances. In Othello the actions of Iago seem plausible because we understand what makes him seek revenge upon Othello. Shakespeare takes care to let us know that Iago wanted the lieutenancy that Othello gave to Cassio and also that Iago suspects Othello of having been intimate with his wife. If we did not understand these promptings, Iago's later actions would seem mere machinations of plot, and Iago's perfidious contrivings are plausible only because we see the hidden impulses from which they have sprung.

To realize how important are motivation and plausibility in the presentation of character one has only to sit through a play in which some character does some deed for which we are utterly unprepared by his former conduct, speech, or position. For instance, the kindly landlord cannot suddenly stamp in and vindictively foreclose the mortgage—not unless he has previously robbed the poor or kicked the dog or given us some other indication of inner cruelty. The miser cannot suddenly begin to hand out largess—not unless we know that he has surreptitiously been feeding the corner newsboy or anonymously subsidizing the superannuated professor. They just wouldn't do those things and the audience would be the first to tell them so. The very fact that we have to draw upon imaginative illustrations instead of calling upon a well-known play for support is the best proof that characters must be motivated or die—and the play die with them. "He doesn't act like himself" and "That's just like him" are accurate observations of human nature, and the play helps to condense time and to speed action by adhering to the homely philosophy of these commonplace observations.

INEVITABILITY. In the adequately motivated character the audience feels the note of what is usually called inevitability, and the dramatist means by "inevitability" exactly what the man in the street means when he says of an individual, "He can't help it: he was born that way," or "Look where he lives and what d'you expect?" That is, the dramatist uses inevitability in the sense of a destiny which cannot be evaded because it is implicit in conditions of personal make-up or of circumstances. Certainly inevitability is rooted in motivation, and motivation is rooted in character, and character was conditioned by circumstance, and circumstance grew from a compounding of events and attitudes. And so we can go on taking apart a dramatic house-that-Jack-built and learn no more than we knew in the beginning—that to understand actions we must probe beneath the surface to the why. Probably "why" is the master key when it comes to unlocking the secret of a dramatic situation. "How" and "when" merely get us through the stage entrance, but without "why" we shall never see behind the scenes.

Naturally there is less feeling of inevitability in a farce than in a serious comedy, for the farce makes more room for chance and fortuitous circumstance while the serious play utilizes the tensions of choice and will. Perhaps there is a small degree of inevitability in character when a clumsy man in a frenzy of embarrassment drops the bottle of scent that he is about to present to the fair object of his affections. But there is much larger inevitability in character when a king lets his wounded vanity betray his common sense. His action has larger implications and may precipitate further rash deeds which shake his kingdom and react to his defeat. Annihilation is inevitable once Faust's supreme desire dominates his action. Ruin is inevitable in Macbeth; it is potential in the ambition of Macbeth and in the will of Lady Macbeth. When one murder did not accomplish Macbeth's purpose he was forced to other murders, driven by the same will to power that motivated his first killing. So also, in *Mourning Becomes Electra*, the mother's suicide is inevitable; it springs from both character and situation and is the certain sequence of her personality in the given circumstances. Less inevitable is the suicide itself in *Death of a Salesman*, but still as we have watched the play we have seen Willy Loman stumbling further and further into inevitable defeat, so that we are in no way surprised when at the end, completely defeated and knowing it, he takes the one way out which presents itself to his numbed mind. To many, the end of Mio in *Winterset* lacks this sense of nothing-else-was-possible; they feel that the shot that kills him comes fortuitously, almost as if the playwright himself has aimed the gun, and so to such persons *Winterset* falls short of ultimate genuineness, no matter how convincing and moving earlier moments of the play may have been.

PRESENT-DAY CONCERN FOR CHARACTER. It is not without significance that the tendency today is to demand character motivation even in farce and melodrama. Although tragedy and comedy have always needed characters to give meaning, the older farce seldom asked how a character came to be the instrument of slapstick circumstance, and the traditional melodrama seldom asked the why of an event. The present-day farce, however, such as *You Can't Take It With You*, is inclined to show motivation through character, and the present-day melodrama, such as *Of Mice and Men*, frequently has the trappings of psychological research. Thus the scientific age imprints itself upon our plays. A century which asks "how" and "why" and "what for" of all its facts and theories, which takes almost nothing on faith, which analyzes its heroes and dissects its values—such an age is bound to carry psychological processes onto the stage in order to make the play seem real. And psychological processes require well defined characters, whatever the mental or social status of the characters may be.

This concern for character, which is today more or less self-conscious, has long been instinctive with dramatists who have something important to say, something timeless, something true. For, dissociated from human values, truth itself is probably as empty as the mythical shot fired in the woods where no one hears. It may exist, but what for? Certainly not for the use of an audience. So the dramatist early learned that arguments are futile things unless warmed by emotion, and that emotion denotes human beings—characters. There is no significant event in itself apart from those to whom or through whom the event happens. It is likely that if all the ramifications of character could be followed to their respective sources the play would be mapped out in perfect diagram because everything, as we have suggested, depends upon, and from, character. But it is just as true, in a different way, that the play depends upon situation.

And if the petty officer feels this way, don't others on the ship probably feel the same way?"

It is just this rousing of interest that is the chief function of the initial situation. If the playwright catches our interest he focuses our attention and so begins to let us see what the play is about. *Hamlet* might have begun with the murder of the king or it might conceivably have begun with the feigned madness of Hamlet but Shakespeare chose that point in the story which he felt best adapted to lead the interest forward to the solution of the play's particular problem. In *The Second Mrs. Tanqueray* the playwright might have toyed with the plan of beginning his play with Tanqueray's proposal of marriage to Paula, or he might have waited until after they were married and living in the country, but Pinero began where he felt he could achieve the maximum of audience interest in his story. In *Mister Roberts*, Heggen might have chosen to begin with an overt action of the captain to reveal a reason for the hostility of the petty officer, but instead he immediately suggests the attitude of the men without benefit of dialogue.

BASIC SITUATION. We approach the play, then, through the initial situation, that particular combination of persons and circumstances which the playwright feels will most surely pique our interest. But behind the initial situation there is a basic situation, that specific maladjustment from which the story rises. In *Hamlet* the basic situation is the murder of Hamlet's father and the hasty marriage of his mother to his uncle. These incidents have occurred several weeks before the incident that opens the play. They make up the basic situation from which springs Hamlet's suspicion, and from his suspicion come his later attitudes which, with their ramifications, are the play. The initial situation and the basic situation rarely coincide but in *The Merchant of Venice* they are the same. It is Antonio's borrowing the money to equip Bassanio as a suitor to Portia that makes the plot that is the play—unless one feels that back of this situation is the enmity between Jew and Gentile as exemplified by Shylock and Antonio.

It is interesting to note how dissimilar playwrights have developed the same basic situation, as in the case of the old story of Paolo and Francesca, perhaps first appearing in Dante's *Divine Comedy*, and subsequently told in different ways by such different playwrights as Boker, Phillips, and D'Annunzio. In fact Maeterlinck might be included since he once wrote to an inquiring student that now that his attention had been called to it he supposed that the genesis of *Pelleas and Melisande* must have been the Paolo and Francesca legend. It is interesting also to note how the going-back-in-time theme has been developed by different playwrights, as for instance by Barrie in *Dear Brutus*, by Dunsany in *If*, and by Anderson in *The Star Wagon*; or how the basic situation of Cleopatra's influence on the Roman world was handled by Shakespeare in *Antony and Cleopatra*, by Dryden in *All for Love*, and by Shaw in *Caesar and Cleopatra*.

It has been said that there are only thirty-six possible situations. Indeed, thirty-six situations have been put into a book and offered to the wishful plotmaker to encourage or discourage his inventiveness. No doubt there must be a limit to the number of fundamental difficulties into which human beings can entangle themselves, but in quite as real a sense there are as many situations as there are playwrights, for characters in a play, like their counterparts in real life, differ in their relationships to one another and to their universe. It is this difference in the reaction of the characters which makes the essential difference in the situation.

Of course it is not necessarily the initial situation or even the basic situation that came first to the playwright's mind. Just as likely he began in the middle of the story, his attention arrested by a peculiar combination of circumstances which had to be accounted for. So it may well have been the tomb scene that first intrigued Shakespeare into developing the story of Romeo and Juliet. With that situation in mind he could have worked back to a basic situation, the enmity between the Capulets and Montagues, and then could have decided upon a logical starting point which became the initial situation. So too *Hamlet* might have risen from the situation of a play within a play wherein an accuser watches the reaction of the accused as he witnesses a reproduction of the crime. With that circumstance in mind the playwright could work backwards to a basic situation and then decide upon an initial situation as the starting point of the play. However, no matter which situation rises first to the playwright's mind he cannot begin the construction of a play until he has found his basic situation. Then and not until then can he begin to see the pattern of his play. And stripped of all pompous terminology, pattern is plot.

PLOT. Plot is contrived from the whole matrix of the story, subjective and objective; the playwright lifts upon the stage such elements of character and event as are necessary for both emotional and intellectual comprehension of the story. These elements become the material for his construction, for his plot. Thus plot is an arrangement of characters in situations, a cumulative progression of incidents.

Just as characters are the raw materials of situations, so situations are the raw materials of plot. The playwright builds to pattern just as surely, although not always so consciously, as an architect builds to pattern. He has a procedure for construction which demands an adroit arrangement of situations so that when his play is finished the onlooker feels unconsciously, and the critic realizes consciously, that each scene should be in no other place than where it is.

For any play the logicality of sequence depends upon the characters from which the story springs and upon the end the playwright has in mind. It is sometimes said that *The Cherry Orchard* "gets nowhere," that it ends exactly where it begins. But that was exactly Chekhov's story—characters so frustrated by circumstances of birth and position that they are powerless to change. His "plotless play" is really a play whose plot is so artfully arranged that events seem to happen, or not to happen, entirely of themselves without contrivance. But if anyone should make a list of the incidents in *The Cherry Orchard* he would probably find that there is no place for any incident except where it stands and that Chekhov put it exactly there with a fine selective apperception. This fitness of the sequence of incidents is more readily seen by most of us in Joshua Logan's *The Wisteria Trees*, partly because Logan has been less subtle than Chekhov was in the original story, but also because the Louisiana setting and American characters and speech are more quickly understood by us. Certainly the static play has plot as surely as melodrama has plot, but it is focused at a different range and under a different light.

SUSPENSE. Naturally the playwright's first aim is to tell his story so that it holds the interest of the audience. The prime ingredient of this necessary attention is suspense. Indeed, it is suspense, the sense of continuing uncertainty, which gives a drama its impetus, for without this "reasonable uncertainty" there is no carry-over from incident to incident. We have all seen plays, alas, which managed to live for a short while without the genuine vitality of suspense. Because of witty lines, or because of lovely settings, or through some hocus-pocus of accident, they land upon a stage and we, the ever-hopeful first-nighters, go forth to see. Expectantly we turn our eyes upon the stage and then, most dreadful of slow deaths, the oxygen of suspense grows thin and thinner, while our attention lapses into the repose preceding coma.

But necessary as it is to the life of a play, suspense is not an element which may be thrown in by the dramatist to manufacture interest. In any valid representation of character in circumstance it already exists, just as it exists in real life all about us, and within us, all the time. There is always the feeling that "something's going to happen," or "something's got to happen," or else the negatives that are themselves a desperate sort of suspense, "nothing will ever happen" and "nothing can ever happen." Perhaps from experience we have no reason to expect that tomorrow will be different, but there is still a chance that it may be different—a chance!—and so for the sake of that chance our days are strung upon the thread of suspense. The individual hopes for progress, for achievement, for triumph, for release, for change of some kind, and his hope is itself suspense. If he were sure that next week, and the next, would unfold in changeless pattern, his suspense would thud heavily to the ground and probably he himself with it. Unless, to be sure, his uncertainty springs from fear that things will not continue to be the same, which is a still more haunting suspense.

When our lives seem eventless—or when they sometimes seem too crowded with events—then we are inclined to turn to the suspense in events about us, to augment our capacity for suspense by feeding it upon events which have small relationship to our immediate concerns. The essence of the newspaper is suspense, and in the main the newspaper's contribution of vicarious uncertainty is probably larger than its contribution of information. Actually, although from the very nature of suspense we do not realize it at the time, we are more interested in speculating whether a team will win or a ticket be elected than we are in their achievements. Certain publicized persons parade through the newspapers, followed by the reading public hanging onto the coattails of suspense: Will he be married? divorced? elected? apprehended? acquitted? It is probably not so important to know as to wonder. For suspense is more thrilling, and sometimes more necessary, than accomplishment. However, this vicarious suspense is more important to us as individuals when the element of intrinsic suspense is largely absent in our own immediate setup. But let our own house catch fire, our own child become ill, our own wife be a candidate for office—in other words, let our own security be shifted into a state of uncertainty, and the serial-story suspense of public events has comparatively little significance.

The dramatist, sensing this human necessity for suspense, uses it as the verity of his play. Indeed, without suspense there can be no play because there is no wonder, no weighing of doubts and uncertainties, there is no carry-over of interest. Moreover, the interest deepens with the actual rooting of suspense in character and circumstance. When suspense is merely festooned on the story, the audience interest lags. For the average theatergoer knows that it is as impossible to get aesthetically excited over contrived suspense as it is to get gastronomically excited over papier-mâché fruit.

Suspense through struggle and conflict. Conflict is one source of suspense. Many consider it the surest source of suspense. At least it is the most obvious. Some observers feel that wherever there is drama there is necessarily conflict, and Ferdinand Brunetière went so far as to say that "the theater in general is nothing but a place for the development of human will, attacking obstacles opposed to it by destiny, fortune, or circumstance." But ever since Brunetière, in the nineties, enunciated his theory of conflict, there has been a good deal of conflict over the enunciation, some drama students defending and others, like William Archer, attacking Brunetière's theory. No doubt some of the argument, pro and contra, is due to a confusion of terms. Those who feel that the terms "struggle" and "conflict" are synonymous, and hoist the dictionary in their own defense, can marshal an array of proof, for most plays do indeed depict some sort of struggle, some opposition to circumstances, some strife. But many feel that conflict denotes a strife in which there is an element of doubt as to the outcome, a chance that the stronger force may, by exertion of will, modify the purpose or nature of the opposition. Those who have this point of view feel that we can have conflict only when there is the possibility of achieving the thing for which we struggle. They would say that mankind struggling against the inevitable, and knowing while it struggles that the result is inevitable, is not mankind in conflict, that an individual frustrated by a force from which he has no recourse and no escape is not an individual in conflict; that, for example, Oedipus, facing an inevitable fate and writhing in mental and physical agony, was not in conflict with the gods. From the beginning they had the upper hand and he knew it. But Prometheus, chained to the rock and struggling with his chains, was in actual conflict with the gods. He could, if he wished, modify the punishment Zeus had meted out to him. His suffering was vicarious in behalf of mankind and before he was thrown into the Tartarus he won the promise of ultimate release. On the other hand, in Strange Interlude Nina is aware from the beginning that her pattern is as set as any decree of the fates: she follows her destiny, struggling occasionally but never with the hope that her will may actually avert inevitable consequences.

Whether or not all drama is built on conflict, one is probably safe in saying that where there is conflict there is almost sure to be drama because where there is conflict there is a doing under tension of will. The conflict may be between one character and another, as in *The Taming of the Shrew*, or between the representatives of opposing classes, as in *Strife*, or it may be between a character and an outside force, as in *Riders to the Sea*, or even between two "minds" within a single character, as in *Hamlet*.

Suspense through obstacles. We have only to look about us to see that a great deal of the suspense in life is furnished by the obstacles that have to be met. "he overcoming of obstacles also requires extension of will and frequently the exercise of considerable ingenuity so that we are required to center both emotional and rational attention upon the thing that prevents our advance. In drama the term "obstacle" is used to indicate any circumstance that blocks the individual's path to his goal. Since uncertainty—suspense—is a prime requisite for the play, the playwright is sometimes tempted to construct obstacles arbitrarily. It is as if he had said, "But the going is getting too easy, I shall erect a boulder in the way"—or an uncle or an intrigue. But when the audience come to the boulder, unfortunately, they are as likely to sit on it to rest and look about them as they are to lend emotional energy to encourage the struggling hero. It is so hard to be convincing against an artificial boulder; the thing collapses without a struggle. We have all seen plays containing these contrived obstacles but we cannot at the moment recall their titles.

On the other hand, it is easy to recall countless illustrations of obstacles in good drama. Macbeth meets a series of obstacles in the individuals who stand between him and his goal. The first obstacle to the consummation of his ambition is the thane of Cawdor, then the king, then Banquo, then Fleance. Gossip is the insurmountable obstacle in *The Great Galeoto*, and credulity the surmountable one in *Spreading the News*. One might say that the toll of the sea is the natural force which forms the obstacle in *Riders to the Sea*. In *Death of a Salesman* Willy Loman's obstacles are his sons Biff and Happy, his employer, his neighbor, who refuse to recognize the false figure of success he has tried to make of himself; and so being unable to face the facts he destroys himself. Indeed, it is impossible to find a play that does not contain obstacles because most plays, like most other stories, can be construed in terms of an attempt to overcome deterring factors, whether in the person of an enemy, or of a parent wishing to forbid the bans, or a force of nature like a rainy day or the implacable power of the sea, or even of a quality within oneself.

Possibly if one really wants to diagram all plays in terms of contentions—struggle, conflict, obstacle, collision, combat, call it what you will—one can make a case for the method. But sometimes the suspense we feel in a play has no relation to conflict, as when we sit expectantly waiting for Mrs. Malaprop to put another word in the wrong place. Or if our suspense is related to conflict, we may not yet be aware of the relationship, as when we see forms silhouetted against the windows in the first act of *The Great Divide*. This is not to say that anyone would wish to deny that the bulk of our suspense in the theater has a definite linking up with conflict, whether it is keyed to such a high comedy note as the expectancy we feel when Lady Windermere says, "If that woman crosses my threshold I shall strike her across the face with this fan," or whether it is keyed to the deeper note of fascination and horror we experience when Macbeth hears the knocking at the gate.

Struggle, conflict, obstacles, these are related to suspense. Indeed, suspense might be called the neural system of the play, efferently connecting characters with action and afferently referring action back to character.

CRISIS. Off the stage it is true that a small amount of suspense will sustain a large amount of monotony. But on the stage, where even a lifetime may be telescoped into three hours, there is no

time for meaningless events. Events in a play are surcharged with
suspense so that the story tends to move from peak to peak, giving
the audience a sense of the intervening valleys without having to
climb down and up again. These peaks of plot are the crises of
the story, and the art of telling a story upon the stage is chiefly
the art of building crises.

A crisis is simply a turning point. It is that moment in the play
when modification is necessary to procedure. The very derivation
of the word—from *krisis*, "to separate"—suggests that the ensuing
development is disjoined from the preceding incidents. Things
cannot go on as they are. Therefore, someone must make a move and
as soon as he does make a move there is a new situation, a different
set of relationships. The crisis is passed, although it probably leads
to another, even more difficult. We may say that a crisis occurs
whenever a character makes a choice which modifies the destiny of
himself or someone else. Doubtless the character is a dominant
one and the choice a matter of some importance. There is not
likely to be a crisis in anyone's affairs when a man chooses to walk
on the left side of the street instead of on the right, even though
that man be a king. But still it is possible that destiny may hang
upon a choice in itself so insignificant. Whether that choice is a
trifling detail or a crisis depends, of course, upon the resultant story.
This sharp focusing of circumstance which we call crisis is one of
the characteristics that distinguish drama from other literary forms.
The leisurely unfolding of pattern and the devolopment of detail
are for the novelist and the poet, but for the dramatist the "planned
tangle" is a necessity.

There is nothing more difficult in all dramatic craftmanship than
the skill of building crises. Almost anyone can think offhand of a
basic situation from which a play might be developed. Conversation
abounds in such remarks as "What a play that would make,"
"They're just like characters in a play," "It sounds more like a
situation in a play," and other phrases which suggest that a given
situation contains the elements of drama. Unfortunately elements

do not combine and develop of themselves: the plotmaker is a contriver and he contrives in terms of crises. In a play there is no room for description for description's sake nor dialogue for the sake of witty repartee, because the play has to telescope emotions and foreshorten intellectual appreciation into the limits of performance on a stage.

Drama also differs from real life most clearly in its treatment of crisis. Frequently we say casually that drama is a representation of real life, and in the sense that it deals with the emotions and choices and values of real life our observation is fair enough. But in real life we can seldom look at a given moment and say, "This is a crisis." Our experiences gather up in varying tensions and rarely draw together sharply. When they do, even when we know that we are indeed in the midst of a crisis, it is still more seldom that we can point to the hour of its dissolution. Our difficulties are likely to drag on, one after another, until some of them wear out and others grow gradually more heavy. In the play a crisis is sharply defined—in order to get ready for the next crisis. The rise and fall of emotions, the tightening and loosing of interest, always in the direction of higher tension, is a necessary procedure for the play.

Naturally there is a distinct correlation between character and crisis. The choice a character makes, whether a Lear, an Elizabeth Champion-Cheney, or a Willy Loman, is conditioned externally by the sort of situation in which he finds himself and conditioned subjectively by the sort of person he is. Manifestly crisis is the product of character and situation continually modifying each other at points where choice is necessary.

The average play is the study of a crisis worked out in terms of ascending and diminishing crises. The opening situation in Sidney Howard's *The Silver Cord* is scarcely set up before we are aware that we are witnessing a crisis. We see Robert Phelps with his fiancée, Hester, whom he has invited to spend the holidays in his home. We see David Phelps arriving with his young wife, Christina, after two years in Europe. Even before the entrance of their mother, we sense that the young men have grown up under her dominance, and as soon as she comes on we know they have never shaken off her dominance and that she means they never shall. The five gather around the tea table and the mother manages with disarming cordiality to make the other women feel that they are in the way. This situation surely foreshadows a crisis. It is a kind of preliminary bout, ominous in its suggestions of what will follow. Choices will have to be made, and soon.

The first crisis comes when Christina and Mrs. Phelps are alone together. Christina insists in a rather casual way that she and David continue their work in New York, he as an architect and she as a research biologist. Mrs. Phelps—although maintaining that she is "only a mother" with no divided interest, nothing in her heart except the well-being of her boys—has already decided that David and Christina are to remain in this the town of David's boyhood where David shall build houses in a new addition while Christina, "if she must have a career," shall have odd hours in the laboratory of the local hospital. As the mother sets her demands over against Christina's plans, we know that further crisis is already imminent and that David will soon be compelled to choose between her decision and the plans he and Christina have made.

The other thread of the story draws taut under the same crisis pattern. Mrs. Phelps's adroit and insinuating questions make Robert begin to doubt Hester's love and to wonder whether he loves her with the intense devotion he has always had for his mother. A crisis is precipitated, Robert breaks off with the bewildered girl. Naturally Christina's honest sympathy is with Hester, and after the others have gone to bed she insists that she and David leave the house when Hester leaves. Emotional intensity increases through a series of crises in which Mrs. Phelps plays for David and Robert's loyalty. Hester, desperate, tries to escape from the house only to fall through the ice on the pond, David rescues her is spite of his mother's restraining cry that he may catch pneumonia, a doctor is called and he tells Robert the truth about his mother's heart attacks which, like her debauches of self-pity, are brought on for effect in an effort to hold her sons to her. Thus, from crisis to crisis the story makes its swift way toward the inevitable final crisis that is the climax: Christina demands David's complete and adult allegiance to their life together in New York or she will go alone. And she wins. As far as David is concerned, the mother is defeated but she wins out with Robert, who cannot extricate himself from the web of her designing self-love. The story is finished, the crises are past, the tensions are resolved.

The Silver Cord is typical of the modern play which presents through a series of crises a major crisis in the life of its central character. Most of Ibsen's plays are of this type, as are O'Neill's *Anna Christie,* Kelly's *Craig's Wife,* Coward's *The Vortex,* Hellman's *The Little Foxes,* and certainly the treatment of a historic crisis is moving and suspenseful in the Cowens's *Family Portrait.*

Theme

IN ITS story sense every play is carried along by characters through crises which are made manifest in conflict, struggle, obstacle, and other uncertainties. Structurally the play proceeds from the initial situation, through development and climax to resolution. But in a third and equally real fashion the play grows from theme.

The theme is the central thought of a play as brought out by the playwright in his story. His treatment of a story springs from his point of view—from his experience, his philosophy—for a playwright, like anyone else, can tell a story only within the compass of his experience and the story is given its characteristic slant by the pattern of his thought.

Sometimes the playwright's attitude is so marked that it becomes a thesis. In such case he is distinctly aware that his play is growing from theme. His thesis is practically a categorical imperative and he chooses characters and situations to make his point, a good deal as a lecturer picks illustrations. But, happily, every playwright does not begin to create his play with a definite thesis in mind. Probably the average playwright is not attempting to convince anyone of anything and certainly he does not intend to persuade to action. He is telling a story because he has a story to tell. If he tells his story well, reaching into the stream of experience, the audience is moved not only by the story itself but by the universal implication behind the story. And probably it is this compounding of the immediacy of emotion with the timelessness of an idea which makes a theme significant.

No doubt all students of the drama agree that a play has some sort of central thought. There is disagreement, though, as to how the theme may be defined. Some feel that theme is the subject, the topic of the play. From that point of view it is easy to specify the theme of almost any play. In that light the theme of Macbeth is ambition, of Othello jealousy, of Romeo and Juliet young love, of A Doll's House marriage. Others feel that theme is a central thought which can be stated declaratively, almost in caption form. Then the theme of Macbeth would be that "ambition o'erleaps itself and falls on the other side"; of Othello, that jealousy devours the jealous as well as his prey; of A Doll's House, that there can be no real marriage without mutual understanding and mutual independence. Those who maintain that theme is subject, however, point out that such statements almost invariably tend to paste a moral onto a play. They also point out that statement runs into story, into situation, and feel that theme is more than epitomized story. Some others lean so far toward story that they set up an entire play in the form of a proposition, as in the case of Camille:

A young man loves a woman of the demimonde.
His father pleads with her to give him up, for his own sake.
What will she do?

The theme of a play is frequently expressed or implied in its title, as in the case of Justice, The Plough and the Stars, Man and the Masses, You Can't Take It With You, What Price Glory, The Adding Machine, As You Desire Me, The Doctor in Spite of Himself, The Lady's Not for Hanging.

Often an observation made by one of the characters in a play sums up the central thought. In The Silver Box, Jones says: "Call this justice? What about 'im? 'E got drunk! 'E took the purse— 'e took the purse but it's 'is money got 'im off—Justice!" In Ghosts, Mrs. Alving says: "I almost think that we are all of us ghosts, Pastor Manders. It is not only what we have inherited from our father and mother that 'walks' in us—it is all sorts of dead ideas and lifeless old beliefs and so forth." In The Circle, Lord Porteous says to Lady Kitty after Elizabeth has gone away with Teddie: "My dear, I don't know that in life it so much matters what you do as what you are. No one can learn by the experience of another because no circumstances are quite the same. If we made rather a hash of things perhaps it was because we were rather trivial people. You can do anything in this world if you are prepared to take the consequences, and consequences depend on character."

Mood

JUST as soon as we begin to consider the attitude of the playwright we find that we are considering mood as well as theme. It
would be as difficult for a playwright to proceed toward building his
play without expressing his mood as it would be for an audience to
see the play without being caught into a mood. Almost at the lift
of the curtain we know, ordinarily, what kind of play we are seeing
and what dominant mood we may expect. For instance, the scene on
the heath that opens *Macbeth* suggests the ominous threat of disaster that broods over the entire play, and the storm gives the play
its emotional pitch just as the prophecy sets the keynote for Macbeth's ambition. In a play of such different temperament as
Charley's Aunt we catch the mood immediately and are conditioned
for laughter in the true farce spirit; *The Green Goddess* has the
mood of melodrama as well as its trappings, and both are almost
instantly apparent; in *Mister Roberts*, as soon as we see the set and
the bored sailors strolling onto it, we know the mood of the play.

More unconsciously than consciously the playwright transfers to
the play his feeling, his reactions, his perspective toward his subject,
and it is this transference which gives a play the quality we call
mood. It may be fairly easy for a student to go through a scene and
find examples of "how the playwright created the mood," but the
student is probably working backwards when he does so. What he
finds is true enough; certain incidents, certain nuances, give to the
scene a sureness of mood sometimes definite and sometimes subtle,
but the playwright did not inject the speech, the action, or the
stage effect to convey the mood; those effects were the natural,

irresistible expression of his own mood. To be sure, in some plays where mood is technical atmosphere or local color we find points at which the playwright has deliberately done something to create his atmosphere; for instance, in *Shore Acres*, Herne had a real horse led onto his stage barnyard to drink real water from a real trough. But that is as far from implicit mood as the play itself is from Maeterlinck's *Pelleas and Melisande* or the same impressionistic playwright's *The Blind*; these are plays of mood and both give us the feeling of a forest, not with literal trees but with the brooding, embracing sense of them.

Almost any play at the beginning strikes its keynote, as we have said, sounds its tone and maintains that tone consistently throughout. If the tone is not consistent throughout, the play goes off key for a time; for instance, during one brief scene in *Shore Acres*, where in the midst of the predominant mood of simple folk in simple relationships Mr. Herne abruptly introduces a thrilling moment of melodrama when the *Liddy Ann* is seen tossing "perilously near the rocks" while Uncle Nat climbs the lighthouse stairs to send the beam out to rescue her. This scene, pleasurable in itself, is as discordant in tone as if Noel Coward were to introduce a scene of homespun virtues into *Private Lives*, or Mr. O'Neill to introduce a heart-of-gold scene into *Desire Under the Elms*.

The Coward and O'Neill titles are sufficient to indicate that mood is by no means always what we imply by the expression "moody," for the mood of *Private Lives* is as brittle as the mood of *Desire Under the Elms* is brooding. We can almost guess as much from the titles before we go into the theater—at least we can guess if we know the playwrights. Even if we do not know the predilections of a Tennessee Williams, we are unlikely to miss the mood of a title such as *A Streetcar Named Desire* or *Summer and Smoke*; and a title as apparently misleading (until we have seen the play) as Lillian Helman's *The Children's Hour* is, in its irony, consistent with the mood of the play. From title to tag mood has much to do with the viewpoint, the outlook, the philosophy of the playwright and producer, as have theme and characters.

Structure of the Play

To MEET the demands of emotional interest, the playwright makes use of suspense and deals with crises as focuses of attention. To meet the demands for information necessary before the emotional interest can be aroused, he contrives his sequence of incidents with an eye to giving us as quickly and as vividly as possible the fundamentals of character and situation.

EXPOSITION. As we have seen, the initial situation shows us who the characters are and what their general circumstances are. But how did they get that way? What is the basic situation that gives rise to these particular relationships? We have to be told the intent of characters and the implications of their circumstances, and the telling is accomplished by what is technically known as exposition. Exposition sets forth what we need to know about the characters and situation before we can understand what the play is about.

By setting. Most of this telling is, of course, accomplished through words and deeds, but a modicum of exposition may be accomplished by the play's setting.

For instance, Ibsen accomplishes considerable before Nora makes her opening remark in *A Doll's House.* There is a comfortable room, tastefully furnished, and Nora coming in from outdoors carrying a number of parcels, followed by a porter carrying a Christmas tree and basket. Before the dialogue begins, the exposition has informed us that a pleasant woman in a pleasant household is preparing to celebrate Christmas.

In *Liliom,* Molnar explains a good deal about his central character by letting us see the amusement park in action, booths, calliope, merry-go-round, a crowd from whom Liliom singles out certain girls for attention and certain men for a scowl, lamplighter unperturbedly lighting the colored lights—all before an intelligible word is caught by the audience.

In *The Cherry Orchard*, Chekhov uses setting, rather than dialogue, to indicate the time of year. When the curtain goes up on the first act we see through the nursery window that the cherry trees are in bloom, while in the last act the trees are stark and bare; likewise in *The Wisteria Trees*, patterned after the Chekhov play, the season of the year is indicated in the first act by wisteria in heavy blossom, then in succeeding scenes by the deep foliage of summer, the sparse leaves of autumn, and the naked sprigs of winter.

By physical action. A considerable amount of exposition is accomplished by means of physical action. Nora's overtipping the servant and her surreptitiously eating candy serve to develop the story, as well as to characterize Nora. Liliom, in Molnar's play, offers nothing but action in the prologue, for the dialogue does not begin until the next scene; he takes an apparent boisterous pleasure in pushing some of the girls through the entrance, he cows certain of their escorts, he mounts his barker's stand and is obviously elated with the scene before him; we know a good deal about the kind of man he is even before he gets into his barker's harangue. Maugham's *The Letter* and Watkins's *Chicago* alike begin with a bang of exposition: a pistol goes off, a woman shooting a man, the story is under way. Less stormy action may also aid exposition. In *Welded*, O'Neill makes use of silent exposition. We see Eleanor lying on a chaise longue, silhouetted against the bookshelves of a dark studio. She picks up a letter from the table, opens and reads it, "an expression of delight and love coming over her face. She kisses the letter impulsively, then gives a gay laugh at herself and falls into a reverie." She has begun her story with wordless action.

Edging it in. Naturally, the most common method of presenting exposition is through dialogue, and there are two chief ways of making such elucidation and commentary. One is the easy method of edging it in so that the spectators are scarcely aware that they are being treated to exposition at all.

For instance, after a silent beginning, Barrie in setting up the opening situation in *What Every Woman Knows* lets us learn incidentally, and yet directly, that Maggie lives with her father and two unmarried brothers, that the brothers have a prosperous business but never had the advantages of education and sorely miss what they have never had, that their books were chosen by the minister who, most inconsiderately, is about to marry another woman than Maggie even after Maggie has embroidered slippers for him. Before she enters we know that Maggie is small, has curly hair, is older than she looks, may possibly never marry, usually has her own way with her menfolk, who turn to her for counsel even as they shower her with gifts. And this in a few short speeches which do not appear to be telling anything.

The obvious method. Then there is the entirely obvious method of presenting exposition. Someone simply tosses the exposition at the audience piece by piece without apology until we know as much as is necessary of the story up to the point where the play begins. In *The Comedy of Errors* the duke's long opening speech explains to the merchant of Syracuse why he is about to be condemned to die. No doubt the merchant knows all about the enmity between Syracuse and Ephesus, all about the possible confiscation of his goods, the forfeiture of his life, and the possibility of ransom. But we in front do not know. Someone must tell us, and so the duke becomes the medium of exposition. The opening speech in *As You Like It* is a large passage of obvious exposition wherein Orlando tells old Adam all those facts about his circumstances which old Adam certainly knows very well—but the play cannot begin until the audience also knows who Orlando is and why he is important. The first and second gentlemen in *Cymbeline* set up the play in direct exposition, one of them telling the other everything necessary to the audience's understanding of the opening situation. Richard III not only characterizes himself in his opening soliloquy but also makes plain his present condition and his purpose. Soliloquy and aside are, no doubt, aids to exposition but so baldly aids that the modern audience largely rejects them or at least demands that they be given the trappings of realism assisted by such accouterments of modernity as the telephone. *The Silver Box* opens with soliloquy but the soliloquy is plausible because motivated by young Barthwick's intoxicated state.

What is the standard for good exposition? Perhaps the final standard is that whatever an audience accepts easily, without resentment, is for that audience good. When two or more characters exchange observations which would be pertinent were there no audience present, then we have an agreeable and persuasive plausibility. The exposition in Pinero's *The Second Mrs. Tanqueray* was called excellent in its heydey, but later was considered too obvious. In contrast the exposition of *Hedda Gabler* was cited as entirely natural. Today many theatergoers feel that the Ibsen exposition also creaks a bit. The fact is that exposition is bound to seem artificial when we examine it closely, for almost always the playwright is compelled to make people in his play say things for the information of an audience which they would never otherwise need to say. It is when a playwright employs a new method that we are inclined to say for a while that his exposition is natural. Then as time goes on and we become familiar with that new method we begin to apply the label "obvious."

In the days when exposition was largely external to the play it was frankly called the prologue, the before-talk. The Euripidean prologue, for instance, spoken by one character in narrative form, provided the audience before the play began with all the facts necessary to the situation. By the time of the French comedies, exposition was gathered into the play, so that the valet told the lady's maid.

Servants, travelers, and confidants. But throughout the history of drama the most faithful servant of exposition has been the Faithful Servant. We have not yet seen and are not likely to see the end of him. The returned traveler has run the faithful servant a close second. Countless plays have had some sort of Rip Van Winkle to help the audience get the news. In the old plays he was rather reticent about his travels but he knew all the questions to ask and listened attentively to the story of what had gone on in his absence.

Another helpful listener in drama is the confidant. In many guises he listens to the exposition, which someone on the stage must listen to in order that the audience may listen in. The confidant is the one to whom past and plans are made known—orally—in such a manner that the audience also is informed. By questions, comment, or raised eyebrows he draws out the story that it is quite necessary we should hear. Sometimes, being properly stuffed with confidences, he disappears from the scene. At other times he turns up—and up and up—to make the confider rue the day. On the stage he is a mechanical necessity just as in real life he is frequently a psychological necessity, and in either case he may be an important person in his own right apart from his role of confidant. Lady Macbeth and her husband are confidants each of the other; Mercutio is Romeo's confidant, as the nurse is Juliet's. These are plausible as well as dramatic uses of the confidant. In a large number of early plays and, alas, in some plays today the confidant seems too especially invited in by the playwright.

The modern method. The modern playwright tries to eliminate purely expository characters and gives to the characters who must explain—or be explained to—a place in the general action. Thus in *A Doll's House,* although Mrs. Linden is largely a utility character appearing out of Nora's past to listen to the story of events which have happened since their last meeting, she also becomes a real part of the play's action. It is she who, through Nora's intercession, is offered the position held by Krogstad, who in turn holds the key to Nora's ruin.

It is all too easy to fall into a common misconception that exposition occurs only at the beginning of a play. Actually exposition runs all through a play. It is needed throughout to develop character and story. Sometimes it is a retrospective bit that gives an added sidelight to enhance our understanding, sometimes it is the on-stage narration of an off-stage action which we need to know about. Almost the whole drama of Ibsen's *Rosmersholm* is retrospective exposition. It comes throughout the play in such cumulative effect that it is the essence of the drama. The actual retrospect through flashback is common today. Rice was one of the first to use it on the stage in *On Trial*, even before American audiences had been conditioned to flashbacks in the cinema. Behrman uses it in *I Know My Love*, going back into the early years of the Chanler family; Miller uses it intermittently throughout *Death of a Salesman*. Whatever its position, exposition has always had the same chief requisite: to clarify both character and situation. When characters forget to make their exposition clear, at whatever point in the play they are expounding, they might just as well go home, for if they do not, the audience will.

Exposition, then, is the means by which we are first told who the characters are and what the situation is. It is the way of letting us understand fully the initial situation, which we see, and the basic situation, from which the play has sprung. Even when the initial and basic situations coincide, we depend upon exposition to give us the information necessary to rouse and hold our interest. Then, once we have the needed information, something must happen which throws the existing arrangement out of equilibrium.

EXCITING FORCE. The factor that is responsible for an imminent upsetting of balance is called the exciting force. It changes the current state of affairs into a state about which something must be done. The ensuing action is the rest of the story. This disarrangement may have occurred before the initial situation, or it may occur at the very moment of the play's beginning, or later. But whatever it is and whenever it occurs, the exciting force is that factor which modifies the adjustment of balance.

For instance, the coming of Anna is the exciting force in *Anna Christie*. The story began long before the opening situation; as early as when the seafaring Chris, who scarcely ever got home, heard that his wife was dead and therefore sent his daughter to be reared by relatives in Minnesota. During the years that have followed, his own life has certainly not been the sort he would want a daughter to share or even to know about. And so, when she suddenly comes back to him, he is compelled to disarrange his customary habits—and companions. Her return is the exciting force of the play. O'Neill picks up the story at a crisis point, her return, and then develops his plot.

In *The Circle* and in *The Twelve-Pound Look*, the exciting force is the return of a woman who ran away from her husband many years before and then one day came back, upsetting the customary relationships.

INCITING MOMENT. The moment the exciting force comes to focus in action, that instant at which the play goes from balance to imbalance, is sometimes called the inciting moment. It is the moment when the play actually begins. Of course, we sometimes feel that the play has begun for us when we enter the theater, or when we hear the first strains of the overture, or when the curtain rises, or when the dialogue begins. But then there comes a moment when we are aware of a heightened interest, of a feeling that "now we're off." This is likely to be the inciting moment, the time when the exciting force takes hold. The rest of the play is the effort to achieve a new equilibrium.

Before the curtain rises on *The Green Goddess*, three brothers of the raja have been taken prisoner and are soon to be executed. This fact makes the exciting force. The inciting moment comes later in the story when the three stranded English travelers first realize they are being held as hostages. At exactly that time the weight of probabilities is shifted beyond the point of balance. In *Macbeth*, the exciting force is the prophecy of the three sisters, but the inciting moment does not occur until Macbeth learns that he is already thane of Cawdor. Then the state that has been exists no longer. New emotions are unleashed. Thought impels to action.

The rest of the play deals with the inevitable disintegration of the character of Macbeth until, through annihilation, a new state of balance is achieved.

DEVELOPMENT. In everyday life it is comparatively easy to start something. Things happen easily, quickly, unexpectedly, and the pattern of a lifetime may be upset by inciting moments, by a too-quick word, a too-slow act, or by a circumstance over which individuals seem to have no control at all. It takes much longer to get out of a difficulty, and on the whole, getting out of trouble is more interesting than getting in. Certainly it takes more ingenuity, more intelligence, more will. And we find in the play too that the development of the problem is the engrossing consideration upon which, pleasantly or unpleasantly, our interest is focused. The development carries the play's main problem through a succession of stages, each preparatory to the next, to the point where resolution becomes a necessity. The ascent of the development—if we think of it in that pictorial fashion—is not an even climb but a zigzag of mounting peaks.

One finds that in discussing a play no matter from what angle, one includes a consideration of development because development is so clearly the body of the play. In discussing the series of crises that Sidney Howard uses in *The Silver Cord*, we have already sketched the development of that play. From the moment the mother engages wits with Christina and Hester for the possession of her sons until the ultimate crisis, when she loses David to Christina, the action has been proceeding with a sure momentum toward that crisis and its culmination. In other words, these actions have been the development of *The Silver Cord*. Again, in repeated references to *Macbeth* the movement of the tragedy has been seen in its development from the beginning of grasping ambition to the beginning of annihilation. And in *The Circle*, from the inciting moment when Teddie Luton says to Elizabeth, "Do you know I'm awfully in love with you?" until the turning of the main crisis when Arnold shouts to Teddie, "Get out, get out, get out!" we have seen the advance to that crisis step by step, action upon augmenting action. Now and then in these progressions there is a pause, as when in the beginning of the third act of The Circle Lord Porteous brings out an album of old photographs to show Elizabeth "what pretty women looked like five-and-thirty years ago"; and as when in the second act of The Silver Cord the family gathers to look at the childhood pictures of David. But these moments of calm merely artfully accentuate the rising action in its zigzag yet always forward-moving course.

In an important sense, development is the play. It is the ascent to climax. It is at once the most gripping part of the play for the audience and the most challenging to the playwright. The challenge which the development presents has given rise to the well-worn pleasantry among novitiates of playwriting, "How's your second act?" For, as almost everyone knows, the modern three-act play may be summarized in a signpost fashion: Act I, Exposition; Act II, Development; Act III, Resolution. The second act is the test of the play, the proof of whether one has a play or not. Plays have survived a weak or not too interesting first act, perhaps few plays have an entirely fulfilling third act, but no play can survive a feeble second act. However, if the second act is convincing, the play may be carried to success in spite of other shortcomings.

On the other hand, a play may easily be imperiled by too good a first act. Moody ran close to the danger line in The Great Divide. Not, in this instance, because the later development was inadequate, but because the initial situation contained such stirring elements of melodrama that an average audience was more prepared for serial-story suspense than for the impact of psychological reaction that was to follow. What saved his play, after a too-interesting start, was his handling of this unexpected development, assisted by Mr. Miller and Miss Anglin's understanding interpretation of the key characters. A better illustration is found in a later play, Raphaelson's Skylark. There the initial situation presents such rich possibilities either of farce complications or of complications arising out of the interplay of temperaments that the playwright never seems quite able to extricate himself from the embarrassment of riches he hands himself—and his audience—in the first act, and it was only the skill of Gertrude Lawrence that carried the play to success.

The development takes the play to the point where the resolution of its problem becomes a necessity.

CLIMAX. Most of us have had the experience of coming to a time when the resolution of our own problems becomes imperative. Sometimes in sudden courage we use surgical methods, sometimes in desperation we run amuck of the regulations that society calls laws, sometimes in despondency we give up in defeat, and occasionally our problems seem to mend without our volition, almost as if they had to get better because they could not get any worse. Afterwards, when the resolution is accomplished, someone looks back to the hour of the breaking point and says, "That was the crisis."

In the play this point of highest tension is the climax. The word is derived from the Greek word meaning "ladder" or "staircase," and it has become a commonplace to refer to the climax of the play as the highest rung of the ladder. But if we are going in for figures of speech, it is more apposite to liken climax to the vantage point at the top of the hill from which we can see on one side the height and manner of our ascent, and on the other the distance but not the means of descent.

Climax in structure. In the earlier five-act plays the climax was generally found at the end of the third act. In the modern three-act form it is found either at the end of the second act or occasionally well into or even toward the end of the third. This high point comes at the end of the second act in *The Circle*, when Arnold orders Teddie out of the house. In *The Admirable Crichton*, a four-act play, the climax occurs at the end of the third act, when the guns of the rescuing ship are sounded, for at this moment Crichton becomes once more the servant, and the tension is broken.

Thus far we have been using climax in its generally accepted technical sense, as Freytag and his disciples used it. If one thinks of a play as susceptible to a diagram, as represented by a scalene triangle, then the apex is certainly the climax. In this geometrical and architectural sense, analyzers have found a definite high point in the construction of every play, a point toward which the rising action is focused and at which the falling action begins. They have frequently described this point as the moment "when all the knots are tied and it is impossible to move further without untying a knot." Thus they find the climax of *Macbeth* in the banquet scene, when Banquo's ghost appears; of *The Merchant of Venice* in the trial scene, when Portia tells Skylock to take his pound of flesh, no more no less; of *The School for Scandal* when Lady Teazle is discovered behind the screen. But they would be compelled to place the climax of *Candida* almost at the finish of the play, when Candida makes her choice. In this way they find the climax by examining the structure of the play to determine the turning point.

Climax in audience tension. But audiences, without giving any name to that moment in the play, recognize it as the moment for which they have been waiting and at which they are at the highest point of theater excitement. Without the aid of a diagram or a definition, to the average audience in a theater a climax is as apparent as a saxophone solo. And today there is a growing tendency to simplify the term "climax" by saying that it is the moment of highest audience tension.

RESOLUTION. When the play has reached its highest height it does exactly what any of us would do after reaching a summit, it starts down again and it comes down faster than it went up. This return to equilibrium is called resolution. As we have seen, the tension ascends through crisis to climax. Then the resolution begins.

The resolution gradually lessens the tension without dissipating the interest. It is the time of approaching balance, like the moment when the finger on a scale oscillates in ever-narrowing margin. Another commonplace expression is to speak of the resolution as the untangling process. To be sure, all the knots cannot be untied with one jerk, for the loosing of certain strands may mean a temporary entanglement in new but lesser tensions. But the movement of the resolution is toward release. The simplest statement of resolution is that it is the procedure of adjusting the difficulties that have made the play.

The compass of the resolution is almost always briefer than that of the first part of the play because it is manifestly more difficult to sustain suspense and interest after the outcome of the story is foreseen. But the play cannot return to earth too suddenly or it is shattered in its landing. Rather, it hits the ground easily, bounces a bit, and taxis to a standstill. In *The Admirable Crichton*, the play may seem essentially finished when the rescuing ship comes in sight, but the act of solution is needed to establish the play's thesis, that caste depends upon environment. In *The Circle*, the resolution starts with the husband's attempt to wheedle his wife. We know then that she is drying her wings for flight. In *Macbeth*, the resolution has begun when Macbeth learns that the murderers have let Banquo's son escape. Circumstances have conspired to defeat the almost unconquerable ambition of Macbeth. It is only a matter of time until he follows his ambition to defeat. In *The Taming of the Shrew*, the solution is under way when Kate begins meekly to pacify and humor Petruchio.

DENOUEMENT. Like the rest of the play, the resolution is made up of a series of situations, a diminuendo of crises, and the situation in which the play finally settles to a position of balance is sometimes called the denouement. The word means exactly what its Latin derivation suggests—the untying of the last knot. If our last question is to be answered, it is the denouement that gives the final answer.

In *The Circle*, we know from the time he comes back for her that Elizabeth is going away with Teddie. At least, we tell ourselves that we are sure of it. With Lady Kitty we say, "Of course the moment he said he'd give her a black eye I knew it was finished." And yet we are not completely sure until Lady Kitty takes off her coat, puts it around Elizabeth, and sends them off to San Michele.

That is the denouement, the moment when our final suspense is satisfied. In *Macbeth*, the denouement is Macbeth's overthrow at the hands of Macduff. In *Mourning Becomes Electra*, it is Lavinia's going into the house of Mannon, there to spend the rest of her days in solitary expiation.

But the modern play tends to have a beginning and a middle, to use Aristotle's terms, but no end in the traditional sense. It tends to follow the pattern of real life, which seldom settles a crisis definitely. Hedda Gabler unties the last knot of her tangled psychology by shooting herself, but Nora walks out to a new life, leaving the audience with the feeling that she has new problems ahead of her, just as an audience feels when, at the conclusion of Odets's *Awake and Sing*, Ralph Berger stands "full and strong" in the doorway. In *Craig's Wife*, the knot is untied for the husband but Harriet is left in the same psychological snarl in which we found her. In *The Cherry Orchard*, we have the feeling that the knots can never be untied in the expected course of things.

The denouement, like the whole resolution, has a note of inevitability, a feeling that consequences are the logical result of what has gone before. The audience is prepared for the denouement. Even though they cannot foretell the specific occurrence that will mark the end of the resolution, when the event occurs it is so much a part of the previous pattern of those particular characters in their circumstances that it seems the expected thing. That is what Owen Davis meant when he remarked that "a playwright writes the first and second acts but in every good play the audience writes the third act."

Terms Used in Play Structure

ALTHOUGH definitions appear to leave little to the imagination, they are reliable springboards from which one can plunge into the broader aspects of a subject. Such starting points are suggested in the following pages, wherein terms ordinarily used in play structure are defined and an attempt is made to sustain the definitions by the precedent of common usage. As in the preceding division, the terms are arranged alphabetically.

ACT. In a general way, of course, everyone knows what an act is. Probably, if asked, the average person would answer that an act is a logical division of the play usually accented objectively by the fall of the curtain. Or he might say that an act is a definite advance forward in the story, a division of plot which has interest unity as well as structure unity. If he tried to be more definite in his answer he would almost certainly run into exceptions, because acts, being divisions of a play, must vary in number, length, form, and purpose according to the style and purpose of the play.

There are two main reasons why a play has acts at all: the playwright has to present his story in stages of action because, plainly enough, continuous action can seldom be depicted in the time and space limitations of a play. Also an audience seems to want at least an occasional breathing spell. Some plays, like Shaw's *Getting Married*, and some productions, like Judith Anderson's production of *Medea*, have tried presentation without intermission, and at the other extreme Mr. O'Neill has twice let an audience go out for dinner during an intermission.

The number of acts a play shall have depends largely upon the purpose and mood of the playwright, modified no doubt by current tendencies. Although the three-act pattern is still dominant, there is a growing tendency toward the stringing together of episodes, somewhat similar in construction to the cinema technique, as is the case in Sidney Howard's *Paths of Glory*, done in seventeen scenes without act divisions, unless a single intermission indicates two acts, or in Vicki Baum's *Grand Hotel*, with its rapidly shifting scenes made possible by a revolving stage, or in Wilder's *Skin of Our Teeth*, which plays in the orchestra pit, on the apron, and on the full stage. It is as impossible to say that a play shall have a given number of acts as to say that a novel shall have a given number of chapters. The play has as many acts as the story has logical divisions which are definite stages in plot advance. A plot which covers a long sweep of time might need more acts than the compact twenty-four-hour play, and the long succession of acts that furthered the purpose of a chronicle play would strangle a high comedy.

We think of the Shakespearean plays, because of the form in which we meet them in the schoolroom, as having five acts, but actually some Shakespeare folios do not show act division at all. The producer frequently determines the acts of a Shakespearean play according to his understanding of and feeling for his production. We say that the Greek plays were not divided into acts but were continuous, yet if we look closely at Greek tragedy we find the equivalent of act division. There is a surging forward of the story, a definite movement which comes to a climax and then is cut off rather sharply from the next dramatic movement by a countermovement of the chorus, which amounts to a "curtain." Even in a motion picture, which normally indicates no act division, we can see where the story is divided into units of action and interest. Several of these movements of continuous action make the picture. Perhaps the closest structural parallel among the art forms is between the play and the symphony, for in both we have divisions according to mood and purpose.

ANTAGONIST. The antagonist in the play is the character who op-

poses most directly the protagonist, or main character. He is adversary to the propelling thought. In *Macbeth*, for instance, the
antagonist is Macduff, in *Hamlet*, Claudius, the usurping king. In
modern discussions of drama the term is less frequently used, although it is perfectly clear that if the term were used we would
speak of the Captain as the antagonist in *Mister Roberts*.

ANTICLIMAX. An anticlimax is a moment of tension which comes
after the climax. In this sense it is part of the resolution of a play
and has a close relationship to the "moment of final suspense," such
as that moment in the third act of *The Circle* when we are uncertain whether Elizabeth is really going to leave, or that instant
just before the final curtain of *The Little Foxes* when we wonder if
Alexandra is wavering in her decision to leave her mother. But
while an anticlimax is technically a secondary climax, serving as a
step-down between the high climax and the denouement, common
usage has tended to give to the term an adverse connotation, so that
we popularly speak of an anticlimax as one which has a tendency to
defeat the implications of the climax or to lessen its effect and are
inclined to feel that the playwright using it has lingered too long
with his climactic effect, a good deal like a lingering guest who
stands too long in the doorway before his exit.

Many modern playwrights have approximated anticlimax in their
determination to carry over into the play the realistic aspect of
ordinary events, which run along indeterminately without benefit of
a curtain on the heels of a climax.

ASIDE. An aside is—perhaps we should say was—a confidential
remark made by one character for the purpose of giving information
to the audience and possibly someone upon the stage, without informing all the participants upon the stage.

Certain modern dramatists have laid bold hands on this method
of exposition and given us the double drama of what their characters
say, expressed in the usual dialogue, and what they think, expressed
in the audible aside. Alice Gerstenberg in *Overtones* elaborated the
technique, allowing the aside to be spoken by separate characters who

personify the real selves of the objective characters, and Eugene O'Neill experimented with the same method in *Days Without End*. O'Neill also used the aside elaborately in *Strange Interlude*, allowing characters to express their thoughts in a monotonous voice which lacks the conventional and emotional coloring of their conversation. But in the main the aside has for a long time been rather taboo. From Ibsen on, the playwright has felt that it is more effective to present the psychological implications of a character as we get them in life, from what a character actually says and does against the background of what we know him to be.

BUSINESS. "Business" is a term more strictly related to the stage than to playwriting because it is a term used to indicate the obvious physical movement that takes place on the stage for the purpose of revealing character, aiding action, or establishing mood. It includes all sorts of movements from here to there and back again, everything from the raising of an eyebrow or the smoking of a cigarette to the smashing of a vase or the firing of a gun. Stage business is often written into the script by the playwright in an endeavor to show the director how the play should be presented, but just as often it is introduced by the director to clarify situation or character. At its best, business is illuminating; at its worst, it is tricky and confusing activity.

Business aids the verisimilitude of a play, making action lifelike, letting us see personality traits through gesture and mannerism, and building the mood in which the play is most convincing. However incidental business may seem, it is never accidental, for the skilled director sees to it that there is no unmotivated movement. The novice, on the other hand, sets his actors to manipulating feather dusters and rearranging flowers as if busyness and business were synonymous. Older manuscripts frequently indicated their authors' faith in all possible directors by merely noting the word "business" without any suggestion as to what that business might be. But too-minute direction for business is even more futile. Actor and director can express through characterization only what they find within the character, so that down to the last movement of the fan in the hands of the least important wallflower business becomes expression of mood or character in physical action.

Similar to stage business are the mechanical effects employed to express the mood of a scene: the storm on the heath, the clashing of swords, the cries of battle in the distance, or even the blizzard in which the errant young mother returns to the old homestead. Even when it is distinctly machine made, such as off-stage thunder, gunfire, radio, or dinner bell, the "effect" is mechanical only in contrivance.

CATASTROPHE. The catastrophe is an event of finality which forces a complete change of plan or intent. Catastrophe means literally to overturn. It is not an incidental change such as the upsetting of a day's plans, but is rather a change which may alter the life purpose, blocking further channels of procedure. In drama the term is sometimes applied to that final action which resolves all difficulties. In this sense it is used to designate the conclusion, the denouement, the unraveling of plot.

The catastrophe may be the debacle of circumstances which are the outward reflection of the debacle of inner values. Such is the death of Macbeth at the end of the play or of Willy Loman in *Death of a Salesman*. Then the event becomes an ultimatum of fate, for there is no righting things, no possible way to restore the former order. In *Julius Caesar* there are two catastrophes, the death of Caesar and the death of Brutus, each marking the end of a career, the termination of a plan, and a high point of crisis in the plot. But death is not the only instrument of fate: shattered health, crumpled hope, loss of confidence, sudden lifting out of the customary social level—these are among the materials of catastrophe, and some modern plays, such as *Ethan Frome*, show a defeated character eking out his days with no such act of extirpation as was granted the protagonists of ancient tragedy.

CHORUS. The chorus was a group of chanters acting as a unit in the more or less passive role of interpreters of the play. In early

Greek drama the chorus had a fixed place in both tragedy and comedy. The Aeschylean chorus used twelve members, the Sophoclean used fifteen, but whatever the number they acted under a leader as one character. Although a part of the play, they were generally extraneous to its action. During the parabasis (the speech in which the chorus moved toward the audience, addressing it in the name of the poet) they often abandoned all reference to the action of the play. In spoken drama today the chorus is seldom seen except in the revival of a Greek play or in an English play based on classical models. In *Mourning Becomes Electra* the gardener becomes commentator and interpreter after the fashion of the Greek chorus. In *Murder in the Cathedral* the women of Canterbury derive from the Greek model, and Eliot has used the chorus device even in a play of contemporary life such as *The Family Reunion*.

COMIC RELIEF. Comic relief is the subordinate inclusion of comedy or even farce in a serious play in order to relieve emotional tension. Such relief is possible in serious plays although it might seem that a little of the genuinely comic would come as the biggest relief in some "comedies."

Most of us are so constituted that we can absorb only a given amount of pure tragedy. We reach a point of tension where our taut nerves refuse to function further. In a play this is the point at which the irresistible force meets the immovable object and we can see no relief for the situation. Then sometimes a play throws in a little comic relief. The porter comes on drunk. For him the censor of intelligence is asleep, and he moves in the happy realm where conflicts vanish like mirages. We in the audience grasp at his mood, we forget, and our deeper emotions are given momentary relief. In the hands of the skilled dramatist, the characters who carry the comic relief may legitimately be a part of the total situation. In the hands of a less skilled dramatist, comic relief is sometimes dragged in by the hair and made to perform antics more grotesque than humorous. In these strained situations the play breaks apart at the joints and the comic relief sticks out like extra elbows. Some think that even the porter scene in Macbeth, although bringing emotional relief, nevertheless articulates obtrusively, and that in The Merchant of Venice Launcelot Gobbo obtrudes unnecessarily.

CURTAIN. "Have we a good curtain?" is one of the first questions a producer is likely to ask, meaning, "Is there effective action immediately preceding the fall of the curtain?" For a good curtain gathers up story, thought, and mood in one exciting moment and all curtains except the final one give a fillip of added suspense, while the final curtain sends the audience home with a sense of completion.

During the years that spanned two generations, a favorite curtain was the picture—they called it a "celestial tableau"—of little Eva among the clouds, surrounded by angels and reaching out her hands to the sainted Uncle Tom. A later popular curtain was the final scene of Shore Acres, when the old man after everyone else has left the stage turns down the lamp, locks the door, banks the fire, muses in the rocking chair, and then goes slowly upstairs, candle in hand. This scene was an innovation and Herne had a hard time convincing the managers that an audience would tolerate such a quiet conclusion. One of the most prolonged curtains of a still later day was E. H. Sothern's conclusion to his production of Hamlet, when Hamlet was borne off the stage with such slow state that the ritual required long minutes, although probably no longer a time than that required two or three decades afterward for the seemingly interminable climbing of stairs that concluded the Olivier screen version of Hamlet. A contrastingly sprightly curtain is that of the penultimate act of Parker's Disraeli, when Disraeli comes so unexpectedly with the threat to close the bank and disgrace the directors that Probert signs the note almost before he knows what he is doing.

PROBERT. There, take your paper, I have signed it. I have signed it to save the bank. It is outrageous that a man like you should have such power.
(Exit.)

CLARISSA (*with joyous enthusiasm*). Oh, Mr. Disraeli, thank God you have such power!

DISRAELI. I haven't, dear child. But he doesn't know that!

THE CURTAIN FALLS.

The best curtains of modern drama are not spectacular, or tricky, or too consciously pictorial. Galsworthy, for instance, brings down the curtain on the first act of *Justice* a few moments after the high point of action, after James How has charged Falder with felony and Falder has exclaimed; "Oh, sir! There's someone—I did it for her. Let me be till tomorrow."

(JAMES *motions with his hand. At that sign of hardness,* FALDER *becomes rigid. Then, turning, he goes out quietly in the detective's grip.* JAMES *follows, stiff and erect.* SWEEDLE, *rushing to the door with open mouth, pursues them through the outer office into the corridor. When they have all disappeared* COKESON *spins completely round and makes a rush for the outer office.*)

COKESON (*hoarsely*). Here! Here! What are we doing? (*There is silence. He takes out his handkerchief and mops the sweat from his face. Going back blindly to his table, sits down, and stares blankly at his lunch.*)

THE CURTAIN FALLS.

In the same play, Galsworthy does not drop his second-act curtain immediately after Falder's conviction but instead shows the court about to hear the next case, and the stage direction is

To cries of "Witnesses in the case of Booley":

THE CURTAIN FALLS.

These curtains illustrate the tendency to show the continuing flow of natural activity after a crisis, just as the less consequential follows the consequential in life.

Many curtains give us the final illumination of character and story. For example, in *Craig's Wife*, Mrs. Craig, who has always "lived to herself" spiritually, is left at last quite alone in the home she has ruined. There we see her plucking the roses to pieces. So convincing, however, has been the characterization that we feel that if we went backstage a few minutes later we should find Mrs. Craig meticulously picking up the petals. Likewise in *Mister Roberts*, the story of the men *vs.* the Captain is accented in the last minute of the play after the news of Roberts's death has been received. Pulver, hitherto such an amusingly tentative character, boldly plucks the Captain's palm trees out by the roots, hurls them overboard, and then defiantly marches into the Captain's cabin.

For the curtain does more than end an act or the play. It leaves a sense of promises fulfilled. A poor house may bring down the curtain, but a good curtain brings down the house.

DEUS EX MACHINA. The term *deus ex machina*, "god from the machine," comes from a device of Greek drama wherein frequently the impersonator of a god actually was lowered by a machine from the logium, to resolve the complications of the play. Today the term is used to indicate a circumstance which artificially intervenes to save action from its logical consequence, and is applied to the device a dramatist resorts to when he is obviously manufacturing a way out. The unmotivated suicide, which resolves a triangle, the parental blessing, where no blessing should be expected, the advance to fortune of the hero, who never did anything to deserve a fortune—these are among the most readily recognized machine-made resolutions. Obvious examples are hard to find in good plays.

ENTRANCE. An entrance is much more than a coming onto the stage. In the theater the term embraces the manner and effectiveness with which an actor comes into the scene. The proficient playwright builds toward this physical entrance so that the entrance scene frequently begins well in advance of the appearance of the actor. Maxwell Anderson, in *Mary of Scotland*, so builds to the entrance of Mary: night, a sheltered corner of a wind-swept pier, expectant guards, the hostile John Knox waiting to speak his mind to the young queen, the stalwart Earl of Bothwell determined that she shall be met according to her royal rank—the ship's arrival, voices along the pier—and then Mary with the Duc de Chatelherault and her four ladies in waiting. Sudermann, in *Magda*, waits until the second act to introduce his main character; Ibsen lets us hear a good deal about Hedda Gabler before we see her; Shakespeare has King Lear preceded by courtiers, by "one bearing a coronet," and by a flair of trumpets.

Now and then a playwright gives his central character no entrance at all but begins the play with the character already on the stage. Richard III is not only on at the beginning but is there alone, Peer Gynt is discovered with his mother, and Faust is seen in his study. Charles Rann Kennedy, in *The Servant in the House*, managed to have his central character on the stage at the lift of the curtain and yet also to give him an entrance later. While we see Manson from the beginning and hear him speak, his back is toward us until—

ROGERS.   What d' you wear them togs for? This ain't India.
MANSON.   People don't always recognize me in anything else. (*He turns for the first time.*)

Similarly, Rostand has Cyrano on stage at the lift of the curtain but we do not realize that he is in the midst of the crowd until later he suddenly discloses himself with such a flourish that the incident is the equivalent of an entrance.

With the advance of modern drama, playwrights—and even actors! —have not always been insistent that an entrance be theatrical. Realism calls frequently for the casual. But even the entrance that gives the sense of the unplanned-for is planned to give exactly that effect.

EPILOGUE. The epilogue is a recapitulation or interpretation of the play after the action is finished. The Greeks used it, with the prologue, as a framework for the total picture.

Sometimes in older drama the epilogue pointed the "moral" or gathered up the ethical implications of the story. Thus in Mrs. Mowatt's *Fashion*, Gertrude steps forth with a final admonition:

GERTRUDE (*to audience*).
> But ere we close the scene, a word with you—
> We charge you answer—Is this picture true?
> Then let the world your honest verdict know,
> Here let us see portrayed its ruling passion,
> And learn to prize at its just value—Fashion.

Sometimes the epilogue merely eased into reality, softening the drop of the final curtain. If the modern play uses the epilogue at all it is usually in the form of an added scene. This is especially true where the prologue presents a problem in a contemporary setting while the play itself reveals the story of an earlier day, as was the case in Edward Sheldon's Romance. Then the epilogue reassembles the characters of the prologue, their experience enriched by the insight that the main body of the play has given them.

EPISODE. An episode is a separate incident within the act. The derivation of the term suggests its origin in Greek tragedy, where the actor literally leaped upon the table to recite his lines between two choric songs. Some use the term synonymously with the French scène to denote an incident during which time, place, and characters are not changed. Others use it to mean the smallest structural unit within a play and they would add that it usually consists of a single incident whose purpose is to reveal character, advance the plot, and create a definite emotional effect upon the audience. They also hold that in every episode after the first some sort of choice is likely to be involved.

EXIT. An exit, although literally the leaving of the stage by one of the characters, dramatically is more than a physical disappearance. Some actors can leave the stage and go home without ever having made an exit so far as the audience is concerned. Others are relinquished so reluctantly that a curtain call is implicit in their leaving—unless, like a Mrs. Fiske, they can sustain illusion so perfectly that the audience never thinks to break the spell by applause. Said Mrs. Fiske, "It is an actor's own fault when he 'gets a hand' on an exit."

The golden day of exits is passed, that day when a character by his calculated withdrawal practically announced, "Now I am about to go . . . now I am going . . . and now [still standing in the doorway] I am gone." In the old-time exit, parting lost none of its flavor and the opening and closing of a door was seldom a casual gesture. This is not to say that the prepared-for slow exit is not found in contemporary drama. Necessarily such departures will always be used by a playwright with an eye to character and the implications of the story he is telling. The slow departure of Blanche Du Bois in A Streetcar Named Desire is poignant and dramatically right, and the picture of her slowly leaving the house, slowly walking up the street as she is led toward the aslyum, is likely to linger with us long after the fall of the final curtain. Even when an exit is necessarily precipitate, the playwright makes the rush from the scene explicitly logical, as Shakespeare did with his banquet scene at the moment Lady Macbeth cries out, "Stand not upon the order of your going, but go at once!" An exit may be a going at once or at long last, but it is always a reasoned going.

FORESHADOWING. Foreshadowing is merely an indication of what is to come. It is indeed the dramatization of the old saying that "coming events cast their shadows before." It is any device, psychological or mechanical, used for preparing the audience to receive, without shock, some further revelation of character or plot. See PREPARATION.

IRONY. In common speech irony is a mode of expression whose intended implication is the opposite of the literal sense of the words. In the play we use the term to denote much this same sort of twisting of purpose. Irony becomes the boomerang of fate, the upsetting of plans which were apparently loaded for success. In The Twelve-Pound Look, Barrie characterizes irony when he speaks of the disquieting occasion of the first wife's return as "that day in your career when everything went wrong just when everything seemed to be superlatively right." Sophocles was keenly ironical in showing characters making preparations to accomplish a definite end and then being finally defeated by those very preparations. Such irony makes the entire situation of Oedipus Rex. See REVERSAL.

PACE. Pace, meaning the speed of movement of a play, is really a term of production. The pace of a performance generally seems to be set by the actor, but back of the actor is the director, who has to carry out the tempo that the playwright found proper for the telling of his story. A considerable part of the director's skill lies in catching this key and "pacing" a performance, just as an expert may regulate a clock whose mechanism might baffle the layman.

Perfection of pace was illustrated through many years in the performances of the Henry Irving-Ellen Terry repertory. Miss Terry was adept at sustaining a staccato tempo and Irving was equally skilled at deliberate timing and the dramatic pause. The Lunts, taking an old familiar play like *The Taming of the Shrew*, made it seem new by their hilarious pacing of it. George M. Cohan, as a producer, was noted for rapid-fire productions and was himself one of the most rapid-fire actors on the American stage. When in later years, however, he came to interpret Nat Miller in *Ah, Wilderness!* his acting was so leisurely and his pauses so long that his own pace dominated the play, although this may not have been the pace that an average director would have considered indicated by Mr. O'Neill's script.

Wrong pacing can ruin a play. It can let a brisk play crawl to the theatrical storehouse or a play of quiet nuances catapult to the same place.

PERIPETEIA. Peripeteia is the Greek word meaning "a sudden turning" and has been anglicized into "peripety," but the more common term is "reversal." In the drama it indicates the sudden about-facing of circumstance, which leads to a result contrary to expectation. See REVERSAL.

PLANT. "Plant" is a term heard more frequently in the theater than in the study and is used to denote the apparently casual insertion of an idea, character, or property to be used more significantly later in the play. Usually when an idea is planted it is called to our attention without undue emphasis, but explicitly enough so that when needed in later developments it does not amaze the audience by its timely arrival. It is started as a seed is, set firmly for growth, and given a chance to root. Certainly if hardy fruits are desired in the third act, the seeds must be planted in the first act, for an audience suspects the genuineness of fruits which suddenly appear suspended in space without tree, root, or vine. A character who is to act heroically in the third act must evince components of heroism earlier in the play. A property which is to be used significantly has to be first brought before our eyes unobtrusively. The gun to be used subsequently is placed in a desk drawer or otherwise incidentally handled so that the audience is aware of its presence and is not deflected from the main line of interest by its sudden disclosure. In Van Druten's *Young Woodley*, one of the boys at teatime casually exclaims about the sharpness of the bread knife so that we are aware of its danger when it is used in the attempted attack later. See FORESHADOWING, PREPARATION.

PREPARATION. Dumas fils once characterized drama as "the art of preparations." Certainly without preparation there is no motivated action, and it is therefore impossible to consider the growth of a play without giving incessant attention to preparation—to the previous arrangement of circumstance, the previous pointing of character, even to the previous placing of properties, all of which have much to do with the reasonableness of the ensuing actions and reactions.

Preparation is germane to the play's development: it is this arranging beforehand for a particular purpose, this compounding for a specific end, which makes action appear to spring from character and move inevitably toward its goal. Preparation is the playwright's method, chiefly by the power of suggestion, of getting us ready for the excitement he is to give us later. It points the way, introduces without ostentation, and predisposes toward easy acceptance. And so running through much of what we have already said about the play, its inception in the playwright's mind, its construction, and its production, has been consideration of preparation. See CHARACTER, MOTIVATION, INEVITABILITY, PLAUSIBILITY—and EXPOSITION, DEVELOPMENT, and in fact almost everything else!

PROLOGUE. The prologue is an adjunct to the drama presented before the rise of the main story. It stands outside the action but

may be a necessary part of the exposition. The Euripidean prologue was spoken in narrative form by one of the characters. Later,
the prologue was presented by two characters, and then by three,
until it was finally absorbed into the main body of the play and
became a part of the exposition preceding the inciting moment.
As is true of nearly all the old devices, the prologue has not disappeared but only gone undercover to reappear in new form; for
instance, in Wilder's Our Town the Stage Manager turns to chat
with the audience from time to time in something of the old
prologue style, as well as playing a part; in Williams's The Glass
Menagerie, Tom follows the same technique; in Van Druten's I
Remember Mama, the function of Katrin is not dissimilar. These
devices are actually as old as the Chinese theater from which they
have been borrowed but they appear as innovations in our day.
Today the prologue, if present at all, is more likely to be an introductory act than an introductory person.

PROTAGONIST. The protagonist in the play is the character who
carries the main thought of the play. His usually is the leading
part in point of motivating the play's action if not the main part
in point of lines. In Macbeth, the protagonists are Macbeth and
Lady Macbeth; in The Silver Cord, the protagonist is Christina;
in Death of a Salesman, the protagonist is Willy Loman.

RECOGNITION. "Recognition" is a term signifying revelation of a
hitherto undiscerned character or fact. A classic example of recognition occurs in Oedipus Rex, wherein the identity of Oedipus is
revealed with horror not only to others but to himself. In Twelfth
Night, the recognition is the physical discovery of Sebastian by
Viola. Or it may be the perception of personality traits, such as
Nora's recognition of her husband, which impels her to say, "I
have been living with a stranger." Or it may be the awareness of a
truth, such as the realization of Macbeth and Lady Macbeth when
they suddenly know themselves for what they are and perceive their
doom for what it is.

REVERSAL. Reversal is a result opposite to that which was intended. Aristotle called it "peripeteia"—a sudden reverse of circumstances. In American history, Burchard's "Rum, Romanism, and Rebellion" speech is said to have brought about a reversal in national politics. So, in literary history, the burning of Tyndale's translation of the Bible in the bishop's bonfire in London effected a reversal, for Parkington, who received a good round price for supplying the Bibles to be burned, sent the money across the Channel to Tyndale, who used it to print more and larger Bibles.

Again, the classic example of reversal is Oedipus Rex, in which the entire plot is built on reversal. When Oedipus is born there is a prophecy that he shall someday kill his father, Laius, and marry his mother, Jocasta. In order to avert that prophecy the child is sent to the mountains to be destroyed, but without his parents' knowledge he is saved by a shepherd. Later he is taken into the household of the king and queen of Corinth and reared as their foster child. Again an oracle prophesies that he will kill his father and marry his mother, and to avert that catastrophe he goes forth from Corinth. He meets Laius at a mountain pass and kills him not knowing his identity. Later he saves Thebes and marries Jocasta. Certainly here is complete reversal of intent and the reversal is completed, dramatically, when Oedipus is finally made aware of his fulfillment of the prophecy.

RHYTHM. Workers in the theater often use the term "rhythm" and know what they mean when they use it, but they find it easier to detect a lack of that quality in a production than to explain what it is when present. Nor are they to be eyed askance for their indefiniteness, because a synthesis of thought and emotion in action is necessarily a variable. We may try to define rhythm and say that it is "a synchronization of the creative energies of playwright, actors, and director in such manner that a unified spirit pervades the whole," but such an expression is only an approximation of what the theater worker means by the expression. Because a play exists only in the moment of its production, we judge it in that moment by its unity, its spontaneous flowing quality, its attention to detail in the spirit of the whole. It is the director who senses and respects each detail of the performance, mechanical or psychic, and sets its rhythm.

SCENARIO. A scenario is an outline of the story of the play. It gives in compact form the content of each scene and act, and indicates the personnel of each episode. The scenario is a scene synopsis, at once an abstract and a summary.

SCENE. The scene is a division of a play during which there is no change of time or place. For people of the stage, "scene" may connote each of the play's high moments. In English drama the word sometimes also accepts the French tradition that a new scene begins whenever another character enters the action, or whenever a character leaves the stage to others. The Shakespearean play tended to use acts of many scenes, sometimes changing both time and place for every incident in the act. The modern drama sometimes goes a step further and presents a play of no acts but many scenes.

SCÈNE-À-FAIRE. "Scène-à-faire" is a term given by the French, always deft at nomenclature, to indicate that scene which the playwright has led his audience to look for, and without which they would feel disappointed if not cheated. The very word indicates that the French dramatists felt that every play contained this "scene which has to be done," and William Archer's translation of the French into "obligatory scene" indicates something of the same feeling. When the playwright has given us characters in juxtaposition, has built up the logic of his plot, and has pointed ever more pointedly to the inevitability of consequences he is next obliged to show us what he has been preparing us for. To do otherwise would be to leave us as flat as if we had gone to the polls only to find a national election arbitrarily called off.

So in *The Silver Cord*, when the issue is drawn between David's mother and his wife, we must then be shown the crisis of that issue when David is forced to choose between them. Sidney Howard gives us that expected scene and makes it the crisis of the play, just as in Shaw's *Candida*, near the close of the play, Candida's choice is the scène-à-faire. Indeed, the scène-à-faire tends to become the climax scene with some of the flavor of well-made play technique.

SOLILOQUY. Soliloquy is a discourse in which the person addresses himself in tones designed to reach the audience. It is the ancient device of the monologue for the purpose of letting the audience know thoughts not articulated for the ear of any other character in the play. Shakespeare made the soliloquy significant for the portrayal of character as well as an adjunct to exposition, but other writers tended to use soliloquy with less skill, letting it become a sort of playwright's oration. Gradually it fell into disuse, if not disrepute, until the telephone came along to rescue it. But this new form, also, has overplayed its part.

In *Strange Interlude*, Eugene O'Neill used soliloquy with asides throughout the play to allow the audience to follow the thought patterns of his characters. Of course there is nothing especially modern about the current avidity for looking behind scenes into the private lives of public persons, but modern man is implemented by his Freuds and his Jungs with a sort of psychological search warrant for prying into remote recesses of motivation, so that an O'Neill soliloquy tends to become a personally conducted tour of a psychological laboratory with each member of the audience a bit nervous lest he himself betray symptoms.

STAGE. The stage in terms of the modern theater is, as everyone knows, the elevated platform, back of the proscenium arch, upon which the play is presented. But "the stage" is no constant term. Perhaps the earliest stage, meaning the place of dramatic celebration, was merely a cleared place before an altar and in this space the acolytes and devotees of the god expressed their propitiation and worship in rhythmic dancing.

We find the classic Greek stage cut into the side of a hill so that the audience might gather conveniently to witness the performance of the dithyrambic choruses at the festival of Dionysus. The dancing place or platform used for the performance protruded well into the audience. Later, as the story element of the play became more prominent, the stage receded from the audience.

In the early days of English drama, when the courtyards of inns were the most popular places for the presentation of plays, the stage reverted to its earlier style and reached out into the audience with spectators on at least three of its sides. Gradually, the more important action of the play tended to occupy the stage behind the proscenium arch while interlocutory bits were presented on the "apron stage"—that unframed portion extending between curtain line and edge of the platform. In general the movement of the stage has been away from the audience, tending more and more toward the presentation of a framed picture, although recently there have been some indications that producers would like again to bring the audience closer to the action. See Part Three, "History of the Drama."

TAG. Every play must come to an end, difficult as it seems to be for some of them to get there, and the last line of a play is called the tag.

Sometimes the tag expresses the theme explicitly in a pointed, or even a poignant, remark, as is the case in *Riders to the Sea*, when Maurya says:

They're all together this time, and the end is come. . . . Michael has a clean burial in the far north, by the grace of the Almighty God. Bartley will have a fine coffin out of the white boards, and a deep grave surely. What more can we want than that? No man at all can be living forever, and we must be satisfied.

Or the entire emotional thrust can be gathered up in a single line. In the last scene of *The Silver Box*, it is Jones who sums up the theme of the play in his bitter comment upon the miscarriage of justice, but it is Mrs. Jones who gathers up the emotional implications of the theme in the last speech of the play, when she helplessly holds out her hands and says merely, "Oh, sir!" Her tag of two monosyllables does more for the play than the long tag of an older day, which was a statement of the "moral," such as Sir Harcourt's speech in *London Assurance*, which concludes with, "The title of gentleman is the only one out of any monarch's gift, yet within the reach of every peasant. It should be engraved by *Truth*—stamped with *Honour*—sealed with *Good-Feeling*—signed *Man*—and enrolled in every true young English heart."

At the end of Barrie's *The Twelve-Pound Look*, Lady Sims epitomizes the theme in a terse comment which is the tag. She remembers the typewriter that had made possible the freedom of Harry's former wife, and after a pause says to her husband:

"Are they very expensive?"
"What?" says Sir Harry.
"Those machines," says Lady Sims.

In that tag she not only recapitulates the spirit of the play but also points a finger toward the future.

Like Rip Van Winkle's toast, some tags summarize a character in a characteristic moment, some give a surprise twist, such as that at the very finish of *Seven Keys to Baldpate*, others are in the nature of an easing down of tension, perhaps sending the audience out with a chuckle after the excitement of a melodrama. Archer accomplishes this easing down when, after the eleventh-hour rescue of Lucilla, he lets us see the raja sigh and hear him say, "Oh, well, she'd probably have been a damned nuisance anyway."

According to stage superstition, this last line is sometimes reserved for opening night and the tag not spoken until the first performance before an audience.

TEMPO. The tempo of a production, as one would surmise from the term itself, is the timing of the play's movement. Timing shares with rhythm the modulation of speech, movement, and pauses into the symmetrical, accentual structure of the play. Now and then one feels that it would be a beneficence if the scripts of plays were marked for their largo, adagio, and allegro passages but since they are not so marked one is compelled to hope that a director will time his performance appropriately. And fortunately, more often than not, he does. See PACE, RHYTHM.

THEATER. In discussions of drama, few words slip more easily into conversation than the word "theater." It is used by some to damn and by others to praise. Those who use it derogatorily feel that the word has a connotation of the artifical, the meretricious, that it suggests trumped-up situations, sensational effects, exaggerated characterizations. Those who use it in praise use it as practically synonymous with "dramatic" and would say that the others mean "theatrical" when they say "theater."

Theater, in its best sense, is that quality which makes a play peculiarly effective as it is produced before an audience, that quality which reaches over into the audience until illusion is complete, resulting in what Pinero called "that peculiar kind of emotional effect the production of which is the one great function of the theater." And since plays are written to be produced, and indeed only exist as they are being presented before an audience, "theater" in this sense is as necessary to the successful play as its title and more necessary than a leading lady.

TRAGIC FLAW. Tragic flaw is that defect in personality which ultimately defeats the individual. This flaw is not necessarily a disagreeable characteristic. In fact, it is quite as likely to be over-agreeability, unreasonable unselfishness, as it is to be a niggardly spirit or an uncontrolled temper. The tragic flaw in Oedipus was rashness; in Macbeth, ambition which "o'erleaps itself"; in Iago, jealousy. Some of us live our whole lives with tragic flaws which never betray themselves as such because circumstances happen to protect us from strain at the point of our weakness. But when the giving way of the tragic flaw involves others with us in possible disaster, then, in the play or out, we have all the material of overt tragedy. See TRAGEDY.

UTILITY CHARACTER. A utility character is a character unnecessary to the main thread of the story but used in some capacity to further the exposition. As far as their own lives go, the main characters in the play could very well get along without the utility character, but the playwright sometimes cannot get along without this character, for he needs just such a person to receive confidences, to ask leading questions, to make discerning comments, and in general to further the characterization of those in whom he is most interested. The better the playwright the less easily a utility character is detected as such. Mrs. Shenstone, in The Circle, is only a utility character. She has nothing to do with the story and is forgotten as soon as she leaves the stage, but while she is on she is very useful in making comments on Lady Kitty's past, and her presence makes more plausible the dramatic presence of Teddie Luton. In somewhat the same way, Nora's old friend Mrs. Linden, in A Doll's House, is a utility character.

Utility characters on the stage are saved from too-great artificiality by the fact that we all use them in our daily lives. They are the friends who always explain the obvious, who ingratiate themselves by recalling the pranks of our youth at a time when we feel the pranks—and the youth—are best forgotten, who display a polite insistence in their indirect questioning as to why the next-door neighbor keeps her front shades drawn, who insist upon having a more intimate concern for our personal affairs than any intimate friend would even suggest. Fine, neighborly people, as a rule, and often quite useful. But nevertheless in the drama of our street they are the utility characters who furnish verisimilitude to their stage counterparts.

THE UNITIES. Aristotle, with his passion for order, laid down in his Poetics definite principles for the composition of drama. Among these was the recommendation, which the Greek playwrights had already fulfilled, that the action of a play should be represented as occurring in one place, within one day, and with nothing irrelevant to the plot. These three unities of time, space, and action are sometimes referred to as the Greek unities, and the rule of the unities dominated tragedy until the freer spirit of seventeenth-century romanticism began to take liberties with both time and space. In modern drama we find only occasionally such a play as *The Servant in the House* abiding by the Greek standards, but all plays maintain a unity of action, even a play such as Shaw's *Back to Methuselah*, spread as it is all over time and space.

UNITY. Since the unities of time and space are generally disregarded by the modern playwright, when we now speak of the unity of a play we mean unity of action achieved in a play's soundness of structure and story, its total impression of wholeness which gathers up plot, character, and dialogue within their frame of time and space so as to present a congruous picture. In a play which realizes unity, all subplots, all subsidiary action, bear in on the main theme so that nothing could be omitted from the play without detracting from its single impression.

In and out of the drama there are sorts and degrees of unity: the unity of the train of cars, of the assembled dynamo, of the tree in bloom. Within the theater there is the unity of the revue, of the chronicle play, of the classical tragedy—many varieties of unity, each depending for its verity upon its use and intent. Whatever its form, the most complete unity absorbs the individuality of its separate parts and presents a single impression. The man who first remarked "You can't see the forest for the trees" would have understood the shortcomings of many plays which appear to have all the elements of satisfactory drama and yet lack that gathering-together which marks a full synthesis.

The lack of unity in the play can have many causes. Sometimes it is the insertion of an incongruous mood, which breaks with the mood of the rest of the play, sometimes it is the intrusion of an unnecessary element, such a passage of sparkling dialogue or an incident which has no connection with the play's action, sometimes it is the appearance of a farcical character in a play which is essentially motivated comedy. When for any reason a play lacks unity, its total impression is an unhappy one. The audience leaves the theater a bit restively. "I don't know why, but the play wasn't so good as I thought it was going to be. . . . I liked it a lot, but . . ." Probably the speakers are confused before a failure which they cannot name but they are unwittingly commenting upon the fact that the play lacked unity.

Man demands from his art forms a sense of fulfillment, which is impossible without the achievement of unity, and so the real dramatist is one who makes the wholeness of his production tell a larger story than the sum of its parts.

THE WELL-MADE PLAY. This is a label applied to drama built to a precise pattern of structure, with situation, exposition, preparation, climax, and denouement deftly manipulated according to fixed laws of play construction. It has at once the advantage and the disadvantage of a perfect mechanical technique. Too frequently the play thus described is too mechanically excellent.

The movement toward the well-made play was headed by Eugène Scribe, Dumas, and other French playwrights of the nineteenth century. The theory is formulated by Francisque Sarcey in his *Essai d'une esthétique de théâtre*. Ibsen learned his lesson in this school and wrote some of his earlier plays to the pattern. Indeed, *A Doll's House*, until the middle of the third act, is a fair sample of the well-made play. Shaw's *Candida* tended to follow the pattern that Shaw himself had ridiculed, but Shaw adds his personality and individual angle of view to the patterned story. Lillian Hellman's *The Little Foxes* is an excellent example of the contemporary well-made play: to the frame of the well-made play she gives the body of her thought and the color of her mood, so that the frame, although there, does not obtrude. It is of course the something more than excellence of construction that makes a play significant. As a matter of fact nearly all good dramatists have well-made plays, in the broader meaning of the term, although they may take wide liberties with the pattern laid down by Scribe. The great dramatist is great because he sees through action to character and through character to motivation. And because his play is the inevitable result of his characters in action, it is well made. In any day, under any formula, a play may abide by all the rules and fail or it may break a great many rules and live, as one quickly realizes when seeing such a play as Sean O'Casey's *Juno and the Paycock*.

PART THREE

History of the Drama

The Drama from Its Beginnings to Today

DRAMA, in its primary sense of action, began as soon as human beings commenced to do things. The singlehanded combat of man with beast is surely drama in the primitive raw. Spoken drama no doubt commenced as soon as human beings had words for their fears, their elations, and their desires. Drama in literature began with the first story. But drama as we think of it today, as something occurring upon a stage in the presence of spectators, commenced at the point where man began to re-act the combat with the beast, when he began to relive his emotions, to retell his story. To be sure, he never re-acted all the action nor retold all the story; he used as much as was necessary to accomplish a desired effect with his audience. It was this selective process which gave his acted story the quality of "theater" and made it drama.

THE FIRST DRAMAS. Those first dramas must have been simple and spontaneous. They have left no written record, but we can rebuild them to a degree from the materials offered by primitive tribes today. Moreover, in certain civilizations, such as the early Greek, we think we are able to see the way in which both tragedy and comedy may have started. Certainly we see more of the beginning process than those early Greeks saw because they were intent upon the primary experience of dancing and singing in joyful celebration of their god of fertility, Dionysus. But sometimes they also danced and chanted with an element of fear in their hearts, for the fields as well as the herds must wait for the blessing of

Dionysus. Obviously it was necessary to keep the powerful god in a genial mood, and how should he be better pleased than by witnessing the sort of entertainment they themselves enjoyed? Nor was Dionysus the only god. There were others as mighty in other relationships and they all needed propitiation and honor. One way of honoring them was to reproduce the stories of their power in the lives of men. And so upon significant occasions groups of actors set apart for that purpose reproduced events, real or imagined, which might be pleasing to the gods. These actors, playing partly for the glory of the gods and partly for the edification of men, impersonated both gods and men. In just this experimental and almost incidental fashion tragedy came upon the stage.

GREEK DRAMA. The Greek stage was not the stage as we know it, neatly fitted into one side of an auditorium. It was merely a space cleared for dancing in the midst of an outside amphitheater. Within the dancing circle there was an altar, and about the circle were tiers of wooden seats built into the hillside. This was the place where people came to celebrate some gala occasion through the ritual of dance and song. Such worship was at least partially spontaneous but part of it was planned beforehand in the form of acted stories. As these "plays" made a larger place for themselves, the actors moved away from the audience so that the dancing circle was no longer in the middle of the amphitheater but at one side. Then in time it became the custom to erect a stage building (the *skene*) immediately back of this acting circle and this building became a background against which the actors played. The inside of the building furnished a dressing room for the actors while the roof served as a waiting place for the gods. From the roof by means of a crane a god could be lifted down to the stage just in time to resolve a dilemma, after which this *deus ex machina* was lifted up again.

The word "tragedy," from *tragos*, meaning goat, may have risen from the fact that the goat was the sacrificial animal used in such celebrations, or it may have risen from the fact that the chorus frequently wore goatskin costumes. Of course the play was rather well defined in form before it was dignified by the name of tragedy.

The beginnings of formal tragedy gather first about the more or less legendary figure of Thespis in the sixth century B.C. He is credited (someone has to be) with being the first actor, the first impersonator of whom it is recorded that he separated himself from the chorus by the importance of his lines, his costumes, and his impersonations. After his time the dancing and chanting of the chorus was broken by one-actor narratives. This one actor in the midst of his performance went into the stage house to change his costume and his mask, and then returned to the stage for another impersonation. Sometimes he carried on a dialogue with the leader of the chorus. Sometimes the chorus answered the actor directly, sometimes they spoke to the audience directly, and sometimes they petitioned the gods directly. Thus the drama of ritual and the drama of story were both upon the stage.

Classic drama began with Aeschylus, soldier, traveler, and playwright (525-456 B.C.). With a growing instinct for theater, he wrote dramas which had more story and less chorus. He added a second actor, and each of the two actors played several parts. Most of the action in his plays occurred off stage to be reported by a messenger, but the dramatist distinctly told a story. To be sure, most of his stories were already known to his audience, for they were the accepted traditions of gods and heroes, but he made them live before their eyes. Through his dramas Aeschylus spoke to the people but he also spoke for the people, interpreting in action their ideas and ideals of justice, sacrifice, and the expiation of sin. A third and then a fourth actor were added in the plays of Sophocles (495?-406 B.C.). More intricacy of plot, more subtlety to characterization, more human interest to themes—these were his contributions to the drama of his day. Euripides, his contemporary (480?-406 B.C.), dealt with the more immediate problems of men, and his drama moved nearer the interests of his audience. Too near sometimes. His flair for championing the unpopular cause and deriding the ways of the demagogue resulted in his being banished, finally, for his unorthodoxy.

Comedy came upon the stage a little later than tragedy, although it probably sprang from the same sort of pantomimic revels in honor of the same patron of fertility, the genial Dionysus. The word comedy is derived from komos, meaning a festal procession. Cavorting in these procession-revels were the masquerading dancers and singers, the clowns, the flute players, the banner bearers, as well as the rhymesters who improvised topical verses to grace the occasion. From the town to the temple the comedians marched and back to their homes again, with buffoonery and antics all the way. By 465 B.C. the comic chorus had marched upon the stage, not yet a raised platform, and had become a regular part of the annual festivals of Athens.

Aristophanes is called the greatest of the playwrights of Old Comedy (444?-380? B.C.). In his hands comedy had dignity, even formality, with its gorgeously costumed chorus of twenty-four actors, its complicated, prescribed structure, its characteristic verse forms. But it also had a timely wit. No one was sacred to the vigorous comic genius of Aristophanes. He took a fling at all things political, at all personages whom the populace honored unduly (or who honored themselves unduly), at the status quo and each of the pillars that supported it, but especially he flayed vice, cowardice, and deceit. Even his most ridiculous situations were made plausible through his acute awareness of the foibles of human nature.

After Old Comedy came Middle Comedy, which was more general in its criticism of current affairs and less vivid in its humor. For us, Middle Comedy is chiefly significant because it fathered so many of the stock characters who have obligingly appeared to mouth lines for the dramatists of succeeding centuries. Menander, its leading exponent, handled the manners of his day with a dexterity which amused even while it raised questions as to basic standards of conduct. His plays, being nearest to the Roman theater in point of time, were freely drawn on for Roman usage.

ROMAN DRAMA. While the Roman theater undoubtedly stemmed from the Grecian, there was also a native Roman drama, in the nature of a crude farce-comedy, in which license exceeded liberty. Among the Etruscans there was a more formal drama which might be considered the link between the Greek and Roman theaters, and it is from the Etruscan word *histro*, meaning actor, that we get our word "histrionic."

The three Roman playwrights whose names stand out above those of their fellows—Plautus, Terence, and Seneca—were less original than their Greek predecessors as creators of character and inventors of plot. Indeed, they freely copied the plots and characterizations of the Greeks, but tempered the Greek propensity for ridicule of political vogue and popular idol to a more general scorn of some of the evils of their day, such as slavery and the amassing of wealth without culture. Also they made freer use of love intrigues and domestic comedy. Beside the three great Roman playwrights stand two great Roman actors, Aesopus in tragedy and Roscius in comedy.

Seneca, once tutor to the young Nero, might have been a greater writer of tragedies had he not been restricted by the fact that there was in Rome no audience for tragic drama. His more serious works had to take the form of dialogues to be recited at banquets, and even in them his clever use of epigram brought more acknowledgment than his sound portrayal of character. Perhaps the greatest glory of the Roman playwrights is their influence upon later European dramatists, who, during the Renaissance, drew generously upon the works of the Romans. The Roman people, although the citizenry came to the theater in unprecedented numbers, preferred the circus and the spectacle to any stage play. A serious dramatist had small chance against the parades of the conquerors who frequently used the huge stages to display their captives in native costumes and sometimes flooded arenas and staged sea battles with real ships. Nor were the gladiatorial combats and the feeding of Christians to the lions any preparation for the subtleties of noble tragedy and fine comedy. The Roman theater gorged itself to death and lay where it fell for the best part of a thousand years.

During those several centuries there were only wandering companies of troubadours and minstrels true to no particular tradition and offering nothing new of any worth. The dramatic sense arose again through the ritual of the church, which lent itself to dramatic celebration.

DRAMA IN THE CHURCH. As Latin fell into the discard as a language of the people, certain of the clergy here and there began to act out the high moments of their religion in order to make the Mass more vivid and to relate it to the experience of the people. These dramatic presentations were built about the great mysteries of the church, especially the birth and death of Jesus, and hence the plays were called "mysteries." Later the miracles of the saints also were dramatized. These plays were called miracle plays. Such legends as The Juggler of Notre Dame made a permanent place for themselves in the lore of drama. Then, as audiences, after some hundreds of years, began to tire of the mysteries and miracles through their misuse, overuse, and abuse, the moralities were added. In these plays virtues and vices were personified so that a theological dualism struggled objectively in the representations of God-and-the-virtues against the Devil-and-his-vices.

In Italy, the religious plays were at first extemporaneous. Then, as the torments of the damned became more and more popular, greater attention was given to plot and structure. A first-class torment needed to be well motivated to be convincing. Frequently real torments were perpetrated and the whole presentation took on the characteristics of the old Roman circus. In Spain, during the thirteenth and fourteenth centuries, the religious play became a gorgeous processional. In Germany, during the fifteenth century, the Meistersinger representing the guilds assisted in the production of the sacred play and sometimes made it a thesis drama, attacking the church.

Conventions of dress and mask, as well as a set procedure for entrance and exit and for certain stage business, helped in finally smothering the religious play. Its long life was partially due, no doubt, to the unity of the feudal system and the unity of the church, both of which made it easy for a play to pass from castle to castle and from church to church. In all Europe the knight and the serf were about equally illiterate and both needed a great deal of bald action to take the place of any literary quality in the play. But, as plays became more lax, the church became more critical until finally drama, which had already moved from altar to porch in the churches, made its way out into the courtyard of the inn.

SECULAR DRAMA. It is seldom, if ever, possible to say at exactly what date one form of drama gives way to another; before one form dies out another has already come to take its place. So we find the pageant coming into prominence in England. The pageant was often an all-day performance of loosely woven stories, each episode generally prepared by a different guild. As time went on, their spontaneity wore thin, as did the imagination behind their contriving, and they became hackneyed, coarse, and anything but religious in spite of their Biblical subject matter.

Strolling players, with their motley collection of traditions, stories, and myths, also went about from town to town selling their wares. Sometimes they were professionals, sometimes citizens acting during carnival season. Or, again, they might be "fool companies" made up of youthful secret societies who took this way of being more outspoken and daring than they could be as their own less colorful selves. Sometimes schools and choirs and even universities offered serious plays on erudite subjects. There is a record that in 1578 the choristers of St. Paul's, London, considering themselves schooled above the average, petitioned Parliament to issue an injunction against "unskilled performers."

There were farces indigenous to every country, which not only borrowed the stock characters from previous generations of playwrights but added the heroes of native folklore. Such were the Robin Hood plays in England. Occasionally in these years a dramatist rose above his fellow dramatists. For instance, Hans Sachs, the shoemaker of Nuremberg who is said to have produced some six thousand plays and episodes, wrote some plays which had individuality and hilarity as well as neat little morals at the end. Puppet shows rose on a wave of popularity which has never completely spent itself. Light one-act plays called interludes became the favorite amusement at banquets or between the heavier acts of a serious play. The masque, whose actors were frequently members of the aristocracy, furnished amusing stories elaborated with singing, ballet, new contrivances in stagecraft, and a great deal of gorgeous costuming.

ITALIAN DRAMA. While most of the varieties of drama were common to all European countries, there were inevitably certain distinctly national contributions. Italy made four such contributions:

The *commedia dell' arte*, a semi-extemporaneous form of drama in which the general outline of a story was plotted, the characters delineated, and then the execution left to the wit and ingenuity of the actors, who really let themselves go in the invention of clever impromptu dialogue and varied impersonations. Not only the actors but also the audience knew the framework of the story so that real skill was required to provide the emotional carry-over. The finer actors brought a discerning appraisal of human nature and a caustic wit to bear upon their rather trite themes. The Italian actor inverted the ancient prerogative of the dramatist to be also his own actor and became his own dramatist. And the play was the richer for the necessity.

Second, the rediscovery of the classic plays of the Romans—Plautus, Terence, and Seneca—and through them of the Greeks. The Renaissance blossomed first in Italy, so that the writers of both tragedy and comedy were handling the Greek structure with dexterity while the English were still laboring along with pageants and chronicles. In drama, Machiavelli, Ariosto, and Aretino are the three remembered names of the fifteenth and sixteenth centuries. Their plays, like the society of which they were a part, abounded in intrigue and connivance, in scandals public and private, in treachery, deceit, elegance, cunning, and profligacy, and the plays, again like the society they depicted, finally wore themselves out in their very excesses.

Italy's third contribution was through the masques, which were an offshoot of the *commedia dell' arte*. Traditional figures about whom gathered certain conventions of mask, dress, line, and characterization found a longtime place for themselves upon the stage: Punchinello, Pantalone, Harlequin, Columbina, and Pierrot, for instance.

The fourth contribution was one which the Italians might have kept to themselves and the drama of Europe been none the poorer —the pastoral play. The pastoral play presented the never-never land of Arcadia where love, lyrics, and lutes take precedence over the responsibilities of a cruel world, where almost anything might happen—and did. But, like most Arcadian dreams, the plays became so sweet that they cloyed the appetites of their workaday audiences. Eventually they slid across the line into burlesque.

Perhaps one other Italian dramatist should be mentioned here: Vincenzo Galilei, whose son Galileo made a science of astronomy. It was Galilei, with a group of friends, who invented a new art form, opera. Galilei and his friends pondered: Why should not the Florentine theater revive the poetical declamation of the Greeks with its musical accompaniment? One good answer might have been that no one had any idea what those musical accompaniments had been. But the Italians saw freedom in the very absence of knowledge and set about making their own musical arrangements. Before that time music had been used within drama, for the masques and pastorals were frequently enlivened with melody, but music as an accompaniment to the spoken line, which gradually forsook the recitative and became an exercise in vocalization, was new. Following these early experiments, the first opera as we know the form was probably *Euridice*, done in 1600 with lyrics by Rinuccini and music by Peri and Caccini. These composers had produced *Dafne* a few years earlier, but the work has been lost to us.

SPANISH DRAMA. In Spain, Columbus was not the only adventurer to push out from the shore at the beginning of the sixteenth century. The dramatists, too, were men of action and daring. They helped themselves to a little of everything they could find—dash and spirit from the troubadours, passion and adventure from the seekers of the Grail, ostentation and grandeur from their Oriental neighbors, terse characterization and compression of dialogue from the current ballads, compact structure from the classicists by way of Italy—all in a compounding of their own devising.

Cervantes, best known for his story *Don Quixote*, also wrote plays, but Lope de Rueda, a Sevillian, was more to the taste of Spanish theatergoers. His was the adroit touch that could make his neighbors mount the stage and do brave deeds the like of which they seldom achieved at home. In other words, he knew the art of persuasive characterization and intricate plot.

But the great name of the sixteenth century in Spain is Lope de Vega. If we know him less well than his English contemporary, Shakespeare, it is not altogether because he was a lesser genius but because his plots and situations have been used so generously by his successors, including Molière, that we call his inventions by other names than his. He often wrote a play a day and still maintained freshness in humor and incident. He used all the popular forms— drama of the cloak and sword; drama which might be called heroic history, in which events and individuals are drawn on a large scale; drama which just misses being comedy of manners by using common-sense common people with the homely touch; and drama of the saints, who lost none of their intrepid daring at his hands. Perhaps he might have overlooked the saints had not Philip II, as part of a wholesale deathbed repentance, proscribed the secular play. With the theater under the ban, Lope de Vega rushed to the rescue and his followers came to know of the pious deeds of the saints in a manner which would probably have surprised the saints themselves.

Even so, he was more truly a creator of religious drama than most of those who came before or after him, for he dealt with the whole of life and left piety in its context of events. Lope de Vega was probably the first romanticist; the first playwright to come out in a large way for the accent on the flair in living. He was inaccurate in setting but accurate in character, he could mix ostentation with warmth and claptrap with feeling. From his day on, the play had a playhouse, and actors had recognition.

After him, Calderón de la Barca gave most to the Spanish stage. He wrote tragedy and comedy, both with the romantic flavor. Ghouls, gnomes, and goblins all came at his bidding and if at times they made his plots a bit absurd they certainly added excitement. He was court poet and bold showman, as well as propounder of amazing theology. But he had a tolerance for human frailty which redeemed the somewhat caustic questioning of circumstance that marked his later plays, and he had an ethical drive which later Spanish dramatists missed. These later dramatists grew extravagant. In the plays that came from their quills dignity became pomposity as plots slipped further and further from character motivation. In spite of variety in material, the romantic play died, or at least went into a trance, to waken again at the close of the eighteenth century. While it sleeps we may cover it with a blanket of its own roses bearing the maxim, "Life is an adventure."

FRENCH DRAMA. Seventeenth-century France, like the rest of Europe, was swept by the Renaissance. Greek ways and Greek plays, diluted by the Latins, seeped into the theater. Alexandre Hardy (to skip the lesser dramatists) wrote five-act Senecan tragedies of merit. He might have the Latin virus but he was honest, he was competent, and—*mirabile dictu!*—he was decent. He was enthusiastic for a newer, freer form of drama, which brought popularity to the Théâtre du Marais, and he wished to be considered a disciple of the nonclassical play. Still, Hardy was a romanticist caught in a net of classicism from which he never quite struggled free.

The foremost dramatists in the tradition of the French theater were Corneille and Racine. Writing in the same period of the seventeenth century, they produced plays which ever since have been standard items in the classic repertory of French actors. Corneille abided by the Aristotelian principles in writing his plays, but preferred politics to love for his themes. The French Academy, established in 1635 by Cardinal Richelieu, accorded him respect both for his notable tragedy, The Cid, and for The Liar, which was the first French comedy of consequence. Racine's genius was for the presentation of love as the most tragic of the passions and the most various in its expression, and he firmly insisted that all tragedy should be motivated by probability. There is evident in his tragedies, such as Phèdre, the stern discipline of construction, and there is a certain austerity to his poetic lines; but they are the discipline and chiseled austerity of a Greek statue. Altogether, he achieved an elegance and a passion which the romanticists of his century never knew.

The French stage of the day was influenced considerably by the French salon, a relationship which was reciprocal but not always advantageous. When the society of the accomplished met in drawing rooms to discuss matters of moment, they had the grace to include the theater among these matters. They called it an Art and gave it Respect, but affectation clouded their judgments until they became attitudinarians. Just as they evaded any mention of the vulgar in their conversation, they demanded the same artificiality in stage dialogue. Of course plays which are denied a draught of the whole of life about them soon gasp for breath. The précieuses (named after the fond address "ma précieuse" with which the ladies greeted one another) in time slipped from criticism to chitchat, so that the respect accorded them by Corneille was turned to ridicule by Molière.

The first half of the seventeenth century was marked for adventure and new beginnings—settlers in America, an English settlement near Bombay, the Dutch on the Gold Coast, Napier inventing logarithms, slaves being brought into Virginia, Sir Walter Raleigh in prison, the Thirty Years' War under way, Gustavus Adolphus heading southward. It was this exciting world with its currents and crosscurrents which was waiting to buffet Jean Baptiste Poquelin, called Molière. And a thorough job of buffeting it did, for Molière was born in poverty and his entire life was a struggle, economic, social, domestic, and literary. He began his dramatic career as an actor, was then a manager, and finally a playwright. It was in 1658 that he came to Paris bringing his own company who had just returned from a ten-year tour of the provinces to play in the Louvre. Molière shares with Shakespeare the honor of not needing to have his plays or his characters listed, for they are our common inheritance. The designs for his plays came from everywhere. Plots he borrowed from Spain, situations from Italy, and anything he could use from the classicists, but he made them his own. His distinction lies in his characterizations, for which contemporary society furnished his materials. Nobles, peasants, priests, doctors, politicians, writers, actors, and all the rest came within the compass of his wit. He was in the court but not of it. Indeed, he was not of any one class and lived and died a very social person who was lonely. His plays include practically all varieties of comedy with some hybrid varieties and they are all distinctly Molière.

After Molière there were more playwrights in France, more theaters, more types of plays. There was peace, relatively speaking; so there was time and energy for the arts. Tragedies that were not unhappy, comedies that were rather sad, with light one-act pieces to fill in the chinks, paved the road between Molière and Voltaire. We leave the French crowds to their own enjoyment while we again cross the Channel to England.

ENGLISH DRAMA. In Elizabeth's England, the masques and moralities had not yet died out. There were also true-crime plays which set the important murders of the day upon the stage and did not spare the gore. There were chronicles given to length and not always free from propaganda. There were romantic comedies, court masques, pastorals, classic tragedies. Certainly there were varieties enough to draw from, but none of the plays was distinguished. Nicholas Udall may be mentioned because he wrote in 1535, approximately, the first English comedy, *Ralph Roister Doister*, classic in style but hardy and fresh in treatment. *Gammer Gurton's Needle*, authorship uncertain, was pure farce, distinguished for the fact that its hilarity, like its characterization, was distinctly English. Thomas Kyd produced *The Spanish Tragedy* and crowded upon the stage a conglomeration of melodramatic devices. There was John Heywood, earlier than the others, but the equal of any in dialogue. There were Lyly, Lodge, Greene, Peele, Nash. And then there was Marlowe.

Christopher Marlowe, imaginative, gifted, and free by his own efforts, should have gone on "scourging kingdoms with his conquering sword," but he was killed at the age of thirty. *Dr. Faustus* and *The Jew of Malta* are tragedies of heroic stature, quite free from the classic mold. What he lacked in humor, in understanding of women, and in quick human perceptions he made up—as nearly as can be done—in grandeur and sweep. His dialogue may lack conciseness, but it was the best blank verse written at that time and he stands at the gate of the great day of English drama.

Which means Shakespeare. When all the answers are in, there is still the riddle of Shakespeare. He happened. For the *where* and *when* we have reasonably accurate data, known to every schoolboy. But *how* is another question. There was nothing in his heredity or early environment to forecast his genius. Yet today he is so drawn upon in the ordinary conversation of ordinary Americans that if we were to delete his epigrams, his quotable phrases, his slang, his jokes, his situations, and most of all his characters, the resulting blank might be his best monument.

Before he became a playwright, he was actor and play doctor. The stage of his day frequently extended out into the courtyard and was surrounded on three sides by spectators, not to mention the fops and nobles who sat upon the stage to be seen by all men and by whatever women dared attend. He knew no subtleties of scenery, because the lines of the play, occasionally assisted by a placard, were the only indication of the scene of the action. His were not the audiences of hushed tones and bated breath; however high their expectancy might climb, his audiences ate and drank *ad lib* through the performance and sometimes played dice and cards. A theater in those days was a place wherein to be amused, and if the actors on the stage did not furnish the amusement the audience used its own ingenuity. Small wonder that a playwright had to be master of the art of invention.

There was no great premium upon originality of incident in Shakespeare's plays; some part of each of them can be traced to its source. Yet the plots are more than the sum of his sources. The social pastimes of Elizabeth's London are reflected in his plots, as are the current attitudes, the foibles and follies of the high and the low. But it is in the faithful and discerning delineation of character that Shakespeare excels. His plays live for us because his characters share the passions, the temptations, the weaknesses, the courage, the humor, and the aspirations that stir and motivate the rest of us. There is significance in the fact that casual historians need say so little about Shakespeare because everyone knows him.

Ben Jonson was brilliant but also pompous. He was best at realistic comedy, for he saw society with both eyes open and he laughed. Beaumont and Fletcher were a lordly pair, and popular. In some chemistry of personality they worked together better than either one worked alone; they balanced humor against pathos; they were poets; they had inventive genius. There were also Middleton and Massinger and others whose distinguished gifts stalled off the day of the theater's closing. But in 1642, after repeated earlier attempts, the English theater was closed and it remained closed for nearly twenty years. The Puritans, inexorable against the pornographic, rebelled also against the merely amusing. There was, too, an element of law-abiding citizenry, less dogmatic than the Puritans, who nevertheless resented the lawless element that the theater's revelries cloaked. Some people were particularly indignant over the taverns associated with the theater, some objected to the traffic jams, and still others credited the theater not only with spreading the plague but with causing it. Altogether the objections were so many that when royalty could no longer be counted on for interest and protection the English dramatists temporarily folded their portfolios and went their separate ways.

When the Stuarts came home from their French exile they revived the English theater, decking it with new regalia. The latest innovation was the introduction of actresses into professional casts for the first time in the history of English drama. There was an influx of French plays and opera under the Stuarts, plus a continuation of Elizabethan drama and a scattering of new plays. Associated with what we have come to call Restoration drama are such names as William Wycherley, with comedies like The Country Wife; William Congreve, with The Way of the World and Love for Love; John Vanbrugh, with The Provok'd Wife; and George Farquhar, with The Beaux' Stratagem. These men wrote wittily of idle gallantry and their plays were comedies of manners. Slightly preceding them, George Etherege had written Love in a Tub, which, produced in 1664, has the distinction of being the first English comedy of manners. Dryden, on the whole a better critic than playwright, was nevertheless a popular contributor to the stage. Among his other plays All for Love, written in the classic form, stands out; for at least a hundred years it was a more popular play than Shakespeare's Antony and Cleopatra, written about the same characters.

With the restoration of the Stuart dynasty to the English throne, drama became something more than a conglomeration of European influence, masked for the English. The Puritans, whose power waned with the Protectorate, continued their attack on the stage with reasons both sound and stupid, but theaters and companies of professional actors multiplied notwithstanding. Drury Lane Theatre, managed during the earlier eighteenth century by Colley Cibber, then for thirty years by David Garrick, and then by Sheridan, gathered together great actors and actresses, among them Garrick himself and Mrs. Oldfield, Mrs. Siddons, and Charles Macklin. The vogue of classicism following Addison's *Cato* was offset in a degree by the spontaneous success of John Gay's *The Beggar's Opera* in 1728. Sentimentality, fresh from France, brought tears, terror, and triviality. But when Oliver Goldsmith wrote *She Stoops to Conquer* in 1773 he brought back something fresh and gay. Goldsmith, too, was sentimental, but he was reviving comedy. Richard Sheridan wrote what was probably the best English play of his century, *The School for Scandal*, which was produced in 1777, a couple of years after his comedy, *The Rivals*. Sheridan's plays were—are—good entertainment and the lines "speak well," as the dialogue of most of the drama of his period did not.

DRAMA ON THE CONTINENT. Across the Channel (a historian must make a good many crossings), Voltaire had been expressing his skepticism in dramatic form. Through fifty years of playwriting this champion of freedom dominated the French scene of the eighteenth century. He drew on faraway localities, South American and Chinese, for unusual effects but in structure he stayed hard by the classical formula except when it cramped his style. With Voltaire, in and out of the drama, the main idea was the drive to free the common people. His plays are today for the most part forgotten, but not his influence.

Alongside Voltaire's play-with-a-moral, France kept the *comédie larmoyante*—the sad comedy—swimming right along in its own tears. And under the tutelage of Diderot, France also managed to provide a sort of perpetual family night of "clean educational plays" which would inspire no one to crime. Nor to anything else. Beaumarchais, less stodgy than some of his contemporaries, presented *The Barber of Seville* and *The Marriage of Figaro*, both later made into operas. French drama of the period not only dominated its own professional stage but also had a numerous amateur following. Mme. de Pompadour diverted Louis XV for years by spectacular court performances; and if we may believe her contemporaries, Marie Antoinette was an actress of merit.

The theater for the Italians had always been exotic, stimulating.

At the turn of the eighteenth century, Vittorio Alfieri, who hated tyranny with an austere hatred, was writing tragedies in the classic mode. Tragedies such as *The Conspiracy of the Pazzi* had passion enough and to spare but could scarcely be called diversion from real life because when Alfieri depicted the Medici in Florence he was only cloaking a picture of his own time. Scipione Maffei's tragedy *Merope*, much admired by Voltaire, is probably the best-remembered play of the period. Metastasio's entertaining librettos had memorable lyric verse as well as sound construction. Carlo Goldoni wrote comedies which, at last, provided laughter through character and situation without the aid of the old broad farce. Some of Goldoni's plays are still on the boards, but at that time they were too "real" for their audiences, who toward the beginning of the nineteenth century turned to Gozzi's magnificent fairy tales, such as *Turandot*.

To the north, Germany was recuperating from war, indeed from many wars, but English comedians brought in Shakespeare, whom the Germans received so hospitably as practically to make of him an adopted son. Italian companies brought Harlequin in his many versions and there he also remained, long after he had worn out his welcome elsewhere under his many aliases. The German theater was not much alive but it was free enough. Even Luther and Zwingli had been favorable to it when there were plays to be encouraged. As the eighteenth century wore to a close, two schools of criticism sprang up, although there was almost no German drama to dispute about. The Leipzig school encouraged new plays after the French classical pattern, while the *Sturm und Drang* (the name borrowed from a play) held out for more imagination and fewer rules. Action, they said, must spring from character, and if action lacks plausibility it is not good drama. These "storm and stress" advocates turned somewhat away from Lessing, whose *Minna von Barnhelm*, rated the first fine comedy in the Germany language, has survived in the theater from the mid-eighteenth century; but perhaps it is for his constructive criticism and his outlining of dramatic principles that Lessing is best remembered.

Then came Johann Wolfgang von Goethe and the critics indeed had something native to discuss. For more than twenty-five years— beginning in the eighteenth and going well into the nineteenth century—this greatest scholar of Europe was director of the court theater at Weimar. But, although he was in the theater, he was first of all philosopher, poet, scholar; and the play was one means of his expression. He wrote tragedies in and out of the classic treatment; *Götz von Berlichingen* presented for the first time a German as the hero of a tragedy. He also wrote comedies, and took side excursions into satire, masque, and operetta. *Faust* is, however, by far the best known of his plays; fifty-seven years went into the composing of this poem-drama. The story had come down from the sixteenth century, enriched by Marlowe's handling in Dr. *Faustus*, but Goethe transcended his sources and recorded his own conception of a soul redeemed by beauty and made wise through suffering. Fully as significant to the German theater as his own plays was Goethe's generous, insistent performance of foreign plays at Weimar. From Sophocles to Shakespeare, he chose the best plays and made his audiences familiar with them. A public so nourished had small appetite for the French sugarplums, artificially colored.

Johann Friedrich von Schiller was another independent German. He felt the struggle for nationalism, he had the German emotional thrust, and both of these speak through the lines of *Wilhelm Tell*.

Germany also had Wagner. Honoring him for his music, we frequently forget what he did for the libretto of opera and for the physical theater. Before him, the music rather than the story or the acting furnished the emotional appeal, but Wagner decided that the plot of opera as well as the score should have a cumulative interest. To illustrate his theory, having learned stagecraft he wrote his own librettos, using the mythology of his own people for his stories. Wagner's methods in the theater were so different from anything the public had been accustomed to that there grew up two elements, one hostile and the other enthusiastic. *Tannhäuser* and *Lohengrin* brought him both fame and exile. During his exile he

worked out the *Ring*; upon his return, under the patronage of the
king of Bavaria he developed the Festal Theater at Bayreuth. This
theater was something new in auditorium design, utilizing for the
first time the sloping floor so that every seatholder was able actually
to witness the action on the stage.

These Germans of the nineteenth century were leaders of the
romantic movement. After them came a group of lesser men neither
romanticists nor yet realists: Heinrich von Kleist, who wrote with
humor of common people; Franz Grillparzer, the Austrian who presented harrowing tales within compact plots; Friedrich Hebbel, who
warned that the drama should teach through action instead of
precept.

THE NINETEENTH-CENTURY ROMANTIC PLAY. It will be remembered that the ultra romantic play fell into slumber somewhere in
Spain toward the close of the seventeenth century. It woke up in
France about the turn of the nineteenth century. Guilbert de
Pixérécourt stood waiting, practically with his pen in hand, for this
revival of interest in the melodrama and added approximately a hundred of the species to the world's collection. Frédéric Soulié, a
younger contemporary, outmurdered and outvillained all the others.
Alfred de Vigny mistook rhetoric for passion and for a while the
public did not object. But given enough crime, even melodrama
will spend itself, and French melodrama of the period had enough.
With it came—and went—its sweet first cousin, the sentimental
drama. Melodrama then as now was essentially an escape device and
France at the close of the Revolution had much to forget.

When one thinks of the romantic school in France one thinks
first of Alexandre Dumas the elder and Victor Hugo. They had a
literary quality which their predecessors lacked and created characters with individuality. Dumas was partial to infidelity as a theme
and served it with trimmings of murder and melancholy in more
than one play. He was a popular collaborator. Indeed, all a play
seemed to need to ensure its success was the name of Alexandre
Dumas for half the signature, even though the collaboration scarcely

went beyond the first great gray tower outlined by lightning against
a distant battlefield. *La Tour de Nesle*, in 1832, was Dumas with all
flags flying. Victor Hugo wrote other plays before *Hernani*, he wrote
other poems, and he made himself a nice new theory about being
"natural" and forgetting the old formalities, but it is in *Hernani* that
the romanticists "burst into full flower." Lovers, villains, honor—
honor to be cherished, lost, revenged—and all the personages of
royal or near-royal status, these are the concerns of *Hernani*.

It is to England that we go for further elaborate romanticism.
Toward the close of the eighteenth century England was a liberal
borrower of German plays, especially those of Kotzebue, an out-and-
out romanticist. The English themselves produced the appalling
and fantastic plays of Lewis and Maturin which Byron and the public at first adored. But it was Bulwer-Lytton who made himself
English romanticist number one. His *Richelieu* and *The Lady of
Lyons* drew crowds in the provinces after more sophisticated theatergoers demanded more humor and less feverish plot contrivance.
An able second to the playwright of his day was Edmund Kean,
the actor, who lived and played with intensity through many mad
years. However, Kean lives to subsequent generations not in his
more romantic parts but in his Shakespearean roles. Macready was
another great actor, great enough to put Byron's poems-in-dialogue
upon the stage, which was more than anyone did for Shelley's *The
Cenci*, the beauty of whose lines did not make up, theatrically, for
its lack of action. To remain in England during the third quarter
of the nineteenth century was to see translations of French plays
on the stage or to sit at home and read the closet drama. Today
we think the armchair would have been our preference, with the
poetic if unactable plays of Tennyson, Browning, Swinburne,
Coleridge, Byron, Wordsworth, Morris, and Arnold. Far removed
from the closet drama were the musical plays of Gilbert and Sullivan, satirists in rhyme and tune and fancy who belong among the
indigenous English dramatists of this period.

Since most of the stage plays of the time came from France, we may as well return there to view them in their native habitat.

Nineteenth-Century France. The first man we meet is Eugène Scribe, the distinguished progenitor of Ibsen's social drama (on the romantic side of the family) and the father of the well-made play. Scribe, today usually read only on assignment, belonged in his own time to the fortunate few whose plays were contracted for in advance, whose income was lordly, whose success was so assured as to be monotonous, and whose achievements merited a seat among the forty Immortals of the French Academy. But one struggles to remember even one of his characters. He had, however, a formula which was mechanically perfect. Melodramas, farces, and some sorts of comedy were sure of arriving if they kept to the track he laid down—crisp dialogue and lively incident clicking rapidly toward a climax. Addicts of the well-made play are still indebted to him.

The younger Dumas came to popularity, which extended as far as America, with the production of La Dame aux camélias. It was a cleverly contrived and theatrically emotional story of "the woman of the demimonde." In his critical essays Dumas fils maintained that it was the purpose of the theater not only to amuse but to "exercise some influence over society." Apparently he considered the social attitude on illicit love the point most in need of reform, for, in plays like Le Demi-Monde, he handled the theme in the grand manner which appealed to his audiences.

Emile Augier, in that he could present human beings, passion and all, without sentimentalizing them, had ability distinguished above his contemporaries. Le Gendre de Monsieur Poirier, a comedy of manners, was probably his best-known work, but Mariage d'Olympe was of larger stature. He accomplished something genuine in showing the essential tawdriness of the misunderstood harlot. Exceptions to the contrary, he felt that there might be a place for such a simple virtue as faithfulness. Scribe outwrote him in the number of his plays, Sardou was more widely popular, but Augier found something in human nature which the others missed.

Victorien Sardou excelled them all when it came to picking just the action, the passion, and idea that would "act well." He used the Scribe form and presented a story with such naturalness that one felt it could never happen thus in real life. He was clever with topical pieces, such as *Divorçons*, but as a social commentator was more clever than discriminating. He substituted facility for reflection and his plays made a fortune—while he was still alive.

THE IBSEN INFLUENCE. Before following the well-made play into England, it is well to trace another influence which was to have a marked effect upon the drama of many nations during the next several decades. This second influence is, of course, Ibsen. Ibsen was schooled in the well-made play and he knew the theater, but the importance of his plays was not in their structural technique. He contributed to the drama of his day an objective social criticism presented in terms of individual experience. To be sure, neither freedom from the old artificialities nor the presentation of social thought was new with Ibsen. In Germany, Hebbel had been caustic in his negative comments upon the current counterfeits of theme, character, plot, and stage devices, and in *Maria Magdalena* he had expressed his convictions positively. In France, Zola also carried his emphasis upon naturalism into a demand for dramatic action which had closer connection with experience. But Ibsen, in Norway, was so deeply resentful against tawdry and unintelligent make-shifts in the conventions of human relationships that his plays shouted their theses in a straightforward fashion which left no room for such old formalities as the aside and the soliloquy. He was craftsman and thinker; he was also a poet.

A list of the themes of the Ibsen plays is an index to the social thought of his day. *Love's Comedy* scorned the accepted hypocrisies of courtship and marriage; *Brand, Emperor and Galilean*, and *Peer Gynt* were the poetic records of men who struggled against their own natures for the possession of their own souls; *The Pillars of Society* was a stern satire on standards of the day, which set most of Europe talking and some of it to thinking; *A Doll's House* showed a woman walking out of a cramped and meaningless marriage with such determination that her footsteps echoed down the decades; *An Enemy of the People* was a bold and even humorous retelling of the story that is as old as Socrates and as new as Ibsen's own experience of a man who would save his people and is himself cast out; *Ghosts* and *Rosmersholm* further italicized his plea for intelligence, education, and courage in social affairs; *The Master Builder* and *When We Dead Awaken* drew upon symbolism and even upon secondary meaning in dialogue in an attempt to provoke insight into the life of the spirit. Throughout his earlier plays Ibsen turned his searchlight onto one after another of the dark areas of society. His later plays tended to move away from social thought to the struggle of the individual against his own nature. Probably Ibsen did not intend such specifics as the emancipation of women, the importance of heredity, and the honest fulfillment of human relationships, to be ends in themselves but rather means toward the realization of something larger, something more essentially free and honest than can be depicted through any one group of individuals in any one set of circumstances.

Ibsen's vitality was typical of a half century during which human society stretched itself with unprecedented vigor. The thoughts of mankind turned outward upon geographical and scientific expansion and inward upon a new effort to understand the mind itself. Those decades spanned by his life covered events as diverse as the development of telegraphic communication, the opening of the Suez Canal, the abolishment of imprisonment for debt, the introduction of vote by ballot, the establishment of national educational laws, the first railway in China, the invention of the rotary turbine engine, the first airship flight, the first celluloid films, the first wireless, the first radio, antiseptic surgery, the discovery of radium, the isolation of the typhoid bacillus, and the beginning of Freudian psychoanalysis. Small wonder that drama began to concern itself with soul searching of an entirely new sort.

Of course, no iconoclast can expect to escape criticism and Ibsen received his full share of calumny. Nevertheless, society was influenced by the infiltration of the ideas and attitudes of the new social drama.

NINETEENTH-CENTURY TREND ON THE CONTINENT. In Sweden, August Strindberg, most intense of the naturalists, wrote such plays as *Master Olaf, The Father*, and *The Countess Julia*. If he believed less in freedom than Ibsen did—indeed, he was opposed to the liberation of women—he was not less vigorous in his denunciations of the ills of society. He seemed driven by the somber idea that happiness must be sacrificed to the attainment of purity, but in such a play as *Swanwhite* he produced delicate and poetic scenes.

In Germany, Gerhardt Hauptmann showed himself a realist in *Before Sunrise* through his manner of depicting personal suffering, and then in *The Weavers* he elaborated both his technique and his social understanding in his presentation of a group of toilers crushed beneath capitalistic greed. *The Sunken Bell* and *Hannele* are plays of a different mood, full of fantasy and symbolic picture. Hermann Sudermann, less poetic than Hauptmann, still carried on the Ibsen tradition of social criticism and was probably at his best in *Magda*, which afforded a great role to the great actresses of his day. Wedekind, Hofmannsthal, and Schnitzler continued the tradition of vivid character portrayal in their dramas.

Among the French writers, Henri Becque took up Zola's advocacy of naturalism and wrote *The Ravens* in a style diametrically opposed to the pattern of the well-made play. Brieux, in plays like *Damaged Goods* and *The Red Robe*, turned social analyst and spared his audiences nothing in his pictures of the social evils. Maurice Maeterlinck, in direct contradiction to the overuse of physical realism, made poetic mood the dominant note in his plays. He scorned the mechanical formula and the hard lessons of burdened society. *The Blind, The Intruder, Sister Beatrice, Pelleas and Melisande*, and *The Blue Bird* all present action within the human soul. Sometimes he dealt with shadowy castles and stark passions, sometimes with talking animals, but the life he presented is not remote from human experience however removed it may be from the daily scene. Edmond Rostand continued the Maeterlinck emphasis upon beauty and nobility of spirit as synonymous with truth and "realism." *L'Aiglon, Chanticler,* and—most of all—*Cyrano de Bergerac* are full of the tragedies that await dreamers, but their wit and life give them a jaunty sort of courage less desperate and more to be coveted in some minds than the large virtues of Ibsen.

DEVELOPMENT OF THE INDEPENDENT THEATER. Not only for playwrights but also for producers, the last two decades of the nineteenth century were a period of experimentation and enlargement. Plays whose content and structure diverged too radically from the accepted norm naturally found themselves with a restricted audience. The commercial manager was wary of the new-style plays and the organized audience was a necessary innovation. Patronage need not be large if it is sure and if it is appreciative of its part in the creation of new standards. André Antoine stands out among the managers of independent theaters. In 1887 he established the *théâtre libre* in Paris. His playhouse was true to its name, and the mechanics of the older classicism and of the outmoded romanticism had no place among his realistic offerings. Like all liberal movements, the free theater sometimes ran to extremes in its attempt to portray every phase of life, but on the whole it contributed a genuine spirit of release to the dramatic awakening that marked the advent of realism. In Germany, *die freie Bühne* sprang up with the same objective of providing an appreciative audience for playwrights who could not conform to the accepted standards of traditional managers. In London, the Independent Theater managed by J. E. Grein offered new plays of realism.

TRANSITION PLAYWRIGHTS. In Italy, the transition writers who dared to deal with the characters and situations of contemporary life were led by Marco Praga, Giuseppe Giacosa, and Giovanni Verga. Praga scorned to believe faithfulness a virtue or to consider its portrayal a valid representation of life. Eleonora Duse increased the popularity of his play *The Enamored Woman*. Probably from the pens of the other two we are best acquainted with the plays that have survived as librettos for operas. Giacosa wrote the librettos for *Tosca* and *La Bohème*, Verga the libretto for *Cavalleria Rusticana*. Gabriele D'Annunzio, although he lacked both humor and quick human sympathy, lives for us in *La Gioconda* and *Francesca da Rimini*. Various other Italians exercised their various proclivities for social drama, psychological plays, comedies, tragedies, and risqué skits; occasionally something crossed the ocean to America. Probably Luigi Pirandello is best known to contemporary audiences, particularly in the plays *Six Characters in Search of an Author*, *Right You Are If You Think You Are*, and *As You Desire Me*. Antithesis is the keyword of his dramatic writing, idea *vs.* event, reality *vs.* illusion.

In Spain also, the flair to be "natural" marked the beginning of this century. José Echegaray's satire on small-town respectability in *The Great Galeoto* was appreciated by English audiences. Linares Rivas, the reformer, Jacinto Benavente, and the Quintero brothers have all done double duty in reacting against the mechanical plot and against the social evils of their time. The turn to symbolic drama and to poetic drama in the plays of such authors as Ramón Goy de la Silva, Jacinto Delgado, Martinez Sierra, and Eduardo Marquina indicated the tendency of later realism, which holds that characters and situations need not lack the aesthetic element in order to be true to life.

BEGINNINGS OF MODERN REALISM IN ENGLAND. For the English theater more than half the nineteenth century was a period of comparative quiescence. There were few noteworthy plays after *She Stoops to Conquer* and *The School for Scandal* in the 1770's. The playhouses were given over almost entirely to rhetorical acting and the spectacle, and only the chief ones such as Drury Lane and Covent Garden were permitted by government license to present legitimate drama. With the licensed theaters thus holding a monopoly, minor theaters sprang up to offer varied entertainment. For the most part, the bills of these variety theaters were not discriminating, and neither were the audiences; or perhaps the audiences determined the entertainment, since, according to Sir Walter Scott, the character of London audiences was such that "no one could have the least pleasure in pleasing them."

But in 1843 the monopolies were abolished and as a result the number of theaters increased. As they increased in numbers they decreased in size, and this aspect of the physical theater, along with the introduction of gaslighting, had a marked influence on the development of stage realism, the smaller and better lighted theater obviously being a more hospitable home for the more intimate plays and acting of the oncoming realism. In the big candlelit auditoriums of the earlier decades there had been plays and actors of the grand manner, indeed many of the actors were not only grand but great and established a tradition which extended from the Keans and Macready to Irving and Tree, but the plays were theatric, written with more attention to the actors' talents than fidelity to character, and they were largely French plays adapted to undiscriminating English taste. And yet, even as early as the thirties, there was a finger pointing toward the future: Mme. Vestris with her burlettas at the little Olympic was anticipating the day of realism by giving more realistic acting and settings, and in 1841 carried these methods to the vast stage of Covent Garden, where she produced Boucicault's *London Assurance* to the admiration of playgoers—an admiration due more to the novelty of presentation than to anything particularly fresh in playwriting. A generation later Squire Bancroft and Marie Wilton, in their renovated and rechristened Prince of Wales's Theatre, sponsored performances which were natural to a still greater degree and in plays that were likewise realistic, for it was in this small theater in 1865 that they produced Tom Robertson's *Society*, and in 1867 the best known of his plays, *Caste*. These plays of Robertson's brought to the stage common people, common subjects, natural speech, natural scenery, and social satire. Innovations indeed, making ready the way for Pinero, Jones, and the English translations of Ibsen.

ADVANCE OF REALISM IN ENGLAND. Pinero was writing plays before the advent of Ibsen's social consciousness, before the techniques of the psychological laboratory. His earlier plays followed the French model in compact structure, terse dialogue, and problems that were stimulating without becoming too probing. But Pinero was craftsman enough continually to adapt his technique to the advancing thought of the day. He maintained that life was an organic whole whose parts were dependent upon and strictly related to one another. Therefore, he strove even in farce to make his characters and circumstances plausible; in fact he practically introduced into English drama the farce of character. *The Second Mrs. Tanqueray* was serious drama geared to the interest of English audiences whose empire building kept them from too much inward analysis. Although in this play and such others as *Mid-Channel* and *Iris* his subjects were contemporary and serious, they neither sprawled into vague generalities nor oversimplified through didactic finalities. With Jones, he worked for the rights of the playwright and for the dignity of the theater. If at this date he seems less penetrating than Ibsen, he was, nonetheless, the interpreter of the life of his times and fellow countrymen.

Henry Arthur Jones was reared in a puritanical atmosphere, never saw a play until he was twenty-one, and grew to be a battler against the puritanical point of view and a foremost playwright. He began playwriting when the Robertsonian formula was still in vogue and finished playwriting among the twentieth-century moderns. Even when he indulged in melodrama he was interested in character and in natural dialogue, and at his hand comedies of manners were again contemporary with the audiences to whom they played. In reviews and upon the platform, Jones campaigned for better plays, better audiences, better producers, and better critics, and he campaigned from the inside out. His plays covered interests as various as the times and probably more adequately reflected the popular mind—including the thoughtful mind—than the plays of any Englishman before his day. *Saints and Sinners* is melodrama but melodrama with a sawtooth edge of satire; *Mrs. Dane's Defense* is comedy but serious comedy; *The Dancing Girl* strikes at intolerance; *The Liars*, at hypocrisy; *Michael and His Lost Angel*, at theoretical morality. But whatever their social intent, the Jones plays and the Pinero plays were entertainment.

Contemporary with Pinero and Jones was William Archer, critic and playwright, whose insistent discrimination helped to cut new channels of social thought for the English theatergoing public. On the other side of the stream of contemporary drama—almost unaware that it was no longer the millpond of romanticism—stood Oscar Wilde. He was not an innovator, not a thinker of the modern social sort. He was a writer of plays in the old form with the old sentimental situations. Only his lines were new, as the dialogue of comedy of manners must appear to be. In *Lady Windermere's Fan* and *The Importance of Being Earnest* his wit was caustic and he jabbed at contemporary society in a way which delighted and entertained that same society. Mme. Bernhardt played his one non-English play, *Salomé*, which had a Continental and American vogue.

George Bernard Shaw not only brought thoughts onto the stage but dramatized the discussion of them, and so sharpened his thought with ridicule that the plays were frequently "extravaganzas of ideas." Being the possessor of a disconcerting sense of perspective and proportion, he saw through the customs and institutions of the day to their intrinsic weaknesses. *Widowers' Houses, Mrs. Warren's Profession, Arms and the Man, Candida, Man and Superman, Caesar and Cleopatra, Saint Joan, Back to Methuselah*—all his plays preached, all provoked argument, and all entertained in spite of a none too facile technique. Shaw advocated character in drama but gave in his own plays fine-spoken puppets. He advocated simplicity but clung to the old formulas. In a day when many thoughtful audiences would rather hear Shaw argue and ridicule, cajole and moralize than buy any other entertainment, they had their wish. And in his plays, his prefaces, and his pronouncements generally he has tried, not without some success, "to make the public reconsider its morals."

Shaw was one of a galaxy, although there were those who considered him a constellation in himself. Granville-Barker, playwright,
actor, and director, was another proponent of realism. John Mase-
field and John Drinkwater brought their gifts of poetry and narration
to the stage. John Galsworthy joined the social crusade of Shaw,
carrying a rapier instead of a megaphone. Whatever his arguments,
they lived in real persons caught into real situations. The current
social problems, opinions, and reactions of his time are presented
under high focus in such plays as *Strife, Justice, Loyalties, The
Silver Box*. His skill as a constructionist and writer of dialogue is
not less in the mellower play *Old English*. The realism of James M.
Barrie is perhaps best individualized by its romantic temper. In
his hands details of temperament, like specific ambitions, are essentials of human nature to be treated with the complete understanding that is humor. His satire is subtle and sometimes keeps
penetrating after the audience goes home. "Whimsical," say critics
and audiences of plays as diverse as *The Admirable Crichton,
What Every Woman Knows, Peter Pan*, and *Shall We Join the
Ladies?*, but it is often a sturdy whimsy, firmly character-bound.

The names of Shaw, Galsworthy, and Barrie still stand at the top
of the list of playwrights who distinguished the dramatic renaissance
in England, which was at its height at about the time of World
War I and came into a slow decline during the years following.
While these three men contributed creatively to the postwar
stage—Shaw, *Saint Joan*; Galsworthy, *Loyalties*; Barrie, *Mary Rose*,
for instance—no new writers appeared to add similar luster to the
picture. To be sure, Maugham's *The Circle* came in the twenties,
but Maugham, too, had been prominent before the war. Between
the wars and afterward interest again swung to the arts of the
theater as differentiated from the art of playwriting—to fine acting,
to impressive production both on the stage and in the cinema, as
illustrated by the acclaim given, on the one hand, to revivals by
the Old Vic Company and, on the other hand, to Laurence Olivier's
Henry V and *Hamlet*, to mention only two instances. Few names
of writers come to mind for inclusion in a brief glance at later

English drama. Probably J. B. Priestley should be named for his experimental covering of many fields in plays as diversified as *Dangerous Corner*, *Johnson over Jordan*, *Laburnum Grove*, *They Came to a City*, and *An Inspector Calls*, and perhaps James Bridie for the mingling of imagination and levity in plays like *Mr. Bolfry*, *The Dragon and the Dove*, and *A Sleeping Clergyman*; and certainly Frederick Lonsdale and Noel Coward, who, like Maugham before them, kept the English comedy of manners up to date.

The only new note in recent English drama has been sounded by the poets, who have supplied this new note by reverting to an older form with, sometimes, a suggestion of contemporary psychology and even psychoanalysis. Toward the turn of the century, Stephen Phillips, in *Paolo and Francesca* and other plays, had attempted to produce poetic drama which would act upon the modern stage, and Gordon Daviot later continued the attempt, although with little modernity and only moderate success. Christopher Fry, however, in such verse plays as *A Phoenix Too Frequent* and *The Lady's Not for Burning*, while using a style which is remindful of Marlowe's in sweep and imagery, adds a humor and satire that spring from today's attitudes, and W. H. Auden and Christopher Isherwood in *The Skin Beneath the Dog* and *The Ascent of F6* have pushed the poetic form further into social and psychological implications with less concern for melody and more for the poetic force of language to express current perplexities. T. S. Eliot (though by birth and early schooling he belongs with the Americans) has turned back toward the Greeks in austerity while being contemporary in thought and reaction, effectively in *Murder in the Cathedral*, less so in *The Family Reunion*, wherein he brings such ancient adjuncts as the Eumenides into the present century. In *The Cocktail Party* he discards the Greek model to push the verse form still further with the accessories of sophisticated English society. Each of these later-day poets, in his own way, is in the vanguard of the countermovement away from literal realism.

MODERN IRISH DRAMA. Modern drama in Ireland was an offshoot —or a taproot?—of Irish nationalism. The movement began with the Irish Literary Theatre, with its interest in Gaelic language and folklore; continued with the Irish Players at the Abbey Theatre, with their emphasis upon Irish actors trained as a repertory company and their ideal of simplicity in speech, acting, and settings; and later in the twentieth century by the sponsors of the Gate Theatre in Dublin, who have carried on the earlier tradition with contemporary modification. William Butler Yeats, Lady Gregory, John Millington Synge, among others, brought their several gifts to the cause in the beginning: *Cathleen ni Houlihan, The Land of Heart's Desire, The Countess Cathleen; Spreading the News, The Workhouse Ward, The Rising of the Moon; In the Shadow of the Glen, Riders to the Sea, The Playboy of the Western World.* After them in point of time are Lennox Robinson, with such plays as *The Whiteheaded Boy* and *The Far-off Hills*; St. John Ervine, with *John Ferguson* and *Jane Clegg*; Lord Dunsany, with *The Gods of the Mountain* and *If*; Sean O'Casey, most notably with *Juno and the Paycock* and *The Plough and the Stars*; Paul Vincent Carroll, with *Shadow and Substance* and *The White Steed*; Denis Johnston, with *The Moon in the Yellow River* and *Weep for the Cyclops*; and some few others, not all adhering to the homely in the particular that had characterized earlier plays, for on the Irish stage as elsewhere there has been a countermovement from the older realism, and O'Casey and others have turned about-face toward the stylized abstract and expressionism.

EARLY AMERICAN DRAMA. Naturally enough, drama in the American colonies derived from the mother countries, and we find it first appearing in Spanish in Mexico City, followed by French drama in Quebec. In the English colonies, drama was just as naturally English drama, and the influence of English drama on the American stage continued for a long time after colonial days. Indeed, it was not until the present century that we became more or less freed from importations and adaptations, and so it is sometimes said that American drama really began in the second decade of the nineteen hundreds.

But this is, of course, only a half truth or a three-quarters truth, because there were early stirrings of a tendency toward something not quite English. In 1766 Rogers's *Ponteach*, published although not performed, began the long succession of Indian characters in our plays. The first real American comedy came in 1787. It was Royall Tyler's *The Contrast*, which, though influenced by *The School for Scandal* and other English models, had an American theme and brought the first Yankee character onto the stage. In 1845 Mrs. Mowatt's *Fashion*, presenting a society woman who parades her riches, mispronounces her French phrases, and mistakes a valet for a count, was successful because of the deftness with which it satirized Americans on the American scene. This play is frequently listed as the first American comedy of manners, but actually several plays antedating *Fashion* had essayed a similar satire, sprinkled with tears and sentiment. Thus American characters began to make themselves apparent, and while they were types rather than individualized subjects, nevertheless they were American. American themes also began to appear. They were superficial themes, certainly, but whether they were treated heroically or satirically, they were reflections of the new country. By the time Aiken dramatized *Uncle Tom's Cabin*, in 1852, and Boucicault produced *The Octoroon*, in 1859, the potent theme of the Negro and race relations, however sketchily or melodramatically it may have been presented, had come to the stage, to be followed through the generations by more and more realistic studies of most of the questions facing a growing nation, from that of "big business" to that of the immigrant laborer.

EARLY AMERICAN ACTORS AND PLAYWRIGHTS. Just as English subjects and characters preceded the American in playwriting, so the English professional actor came before there were American professional actors. But beginning with Edwin Forrest, who was the first great American actor—playing for nearly half a century during those decades between the eighteen-twenties and the eighteen-seventies, when expansion of travel was also providing the expansion of the theater—there was an increasing number of native-born actors to supplant the visitors. The first professional playwright in America was William Dunlap, who wrote or adapted a variety of plays with cosmopolitan settings and materials, controlled the chief theater circuit for fifteen years, was associated with the early literary clubs, wrote in 1832 the first history of the American theater, and is said to have been the first American manager to "give the public what it wants."

REALISM IN AMERICAN DRAMA. The new note in drama toward the end of the nineteenth and into the twentieth century was, of course, realism. This preoccupation with reality came slowly, edging out the artificialities of the previously accepted forms. There had been first the realism of settings, then the realism of characterization, and later the realism of subject or thought. The "local color" plays, for instance, presented very realistic details of setting, properties, and all the other affectations of the locale. A little later came more genuine characterization; still, however, a surface realism. The feeling after reality in environment and characterization is illustrated in most of the plays of James A. Herne. *Shore Acres* had all the homespun accessories of actual life on the farm, as did Denman Thompson's *The Old Homestead*. This outer realism served to prepare the way for the twentieth-century psychological realism in much the same manner that the plays of Robertson had prepared the way for the later Ibsen-Jones-Pinero period in England. Realistic thought came later. Indeed, Herne's *Margaret Flemming*, today considered his most "advanced" play, was not successful because it was too real in thought, and *Griffith Davenport*, his Civil War play, did not succeed for the same reason.

In contemplating the advance of realism it is easy not to give enough credit to David Belasco, yet the significance of his realistic productions was not small, for through them audiences became accustomed to expecting surface realism and hence were ready for and demanded deeper realism later. Both Clyde Fitch and Augustus Thomas, with plays like Fitch's *The Girl with the Green Eyes*, *The Truth*, *The City*, and Thomas's *As a Man Thinks* and *The Witching Hour*, showed the advance toward this deeper awareness. These men reflected the manners and something of the thought patterns of their day. Like Jones and Pinero, they kept fluid the materials of drama and deepened the channels of dramatic appreciation.

AMERICAN DRAMA SINCE 1914. It was not until around 1914 that America began to have truly indigenous plays. In the twentieth century, in America as in England, the influence of the independent theater began to be felt. The organizations we hear most of on this side of the Atlantic are the Provincetown Players and the Washington Square Players, the latter of which ultimately grew into the New York Theater Guild. It was the Provincetown Players who gave first production to Eugene O'Neill's first plays. Perhaps it is not far from the truth to say that real American drama began that night at the Wharf Theater in Provincetown when the first O'Neill audience heard the water lapping under the floor of the theater while *Bound East for Cardiff* was being enacted for the first time on any stage. In this simple manner under the auspices of an independent theater began the career of a playwright who is generally considered the foremost American dramatist. He does not restrict his plays to the presentation of any particularized American attitude. Instead, he draws human beings more than life size against a background of common experience, disclosing motivations as old as organized society and uncovering fears and desires still older, both in his most successful dramas, *Desire Under the Elms* and *Mourning Becomes Electra*, and in his later and less convincing play, *The Iceman Cometh*.

Since 1914, playwrights of the American scene and theme have been numerous. Among them are George Kelly, with his pictures of suburbia, Philip Barry, with his sophisticates of Park Avenue and the other avenues, Elmer Rice and Clifford Odets, with their city proletarians, Lynn Riggs, with his Southwest cowboys, and Paul Green, with his Carolinian whites and blacks. Ever since Langdon Mitchell's *The New York Idea*, in 1906, we have had plays interpreting our national life in terms of satire, while, on the other hand, Sidney Howard, in plays like *The Silver Cord* and *They Knew What They Wanted*, uncovers motivations in terms of the modern psychology, Maxwell Anderson in poetic or semipoetic form presents Americans of today in *Winterset* and of today and yesterday in *High Tor*, Lillian Hellman explores individual psychologies and national perils in such a tightly constructed play as *The Little Foxes*. Robert Sherwood looks at international perils in such similarly well-constructed plays as *Idiot's Delight* and *There Shall Be No Night*; Arthur Miller shows the frustrations of baffled mediocrity in such a semi-impressionistic play as *Death of a Salesman*. *What Price Glory*, arresting, even shocking in 1924, is typical of the war play that beats at complacency, and later plays like *Command Decision* and *Mister Roberts* present backgrounds of World War II with similar techniques of realism. But here as elsewhere certain playwrights have felt restless in the presence of the older realism (so new such a short time ago) and have been reaching out for ways of saying the truth as they see it without the minutiae of scenic realism. Whether with a revue pattern, as in *The Cradle Will Rock*, or a disregard of conventional scenery, as in Wilder's *Our Town* and Williams's *The Glass Menagerie*, or with a thrust into expressionism, as in Irwin Shaw's *Bury the Dead*, they have marked a minority impulse which if not unique is at least fresh in spirit and awareness.

TRENDS IN CONTEMPORARY DRAMA. The new and the old still mingle in the theater of the Western world. In Germany, the newer note has been sounded by men like Ernst Toller and Georg Kaiser, in such expressionistic plays respectively as *Man and the Masses* and *From Morn to Midnight*. In France, form and style have persisted, although with recurring minor revolutions from the traditional; Giraudoux, in *Amphitryon 38*, and Deval, in

Tovarich, are decidedly in the French tradition, while Sartre, in existentialist plays like *The Flies* and *No Exit*, illustrates a veering away from the established type. Spain has contributed relatively little to the drama of today, except for the plays of Garcia-Lorca, which have drawn appreciable attention. Russia, coming so late into the field of world drama and becoming so suddenly great under the impetus of Stanislavsky in production and Chekhov, Tolstoi, Gorky, Andreev, and a few others in playwriting, has in the Soviet theater channeled its energy chiefly into patriotic propaganda by writers such as Afinagenov, Korneichuk, Leonov, and Simonov. Probably in this period of world adjustments both here and abroad new writers with new viewpoints, and new producers to give them a hearing, are in the offing. We can only wait to see.

PART FOUR

Dictionary of Terms and Indexes

A Dictionary of Terms Used in Playwriting and Production

As WE have said in the Introduction, the reader may stand definitions up like a row of tenpins to be shot at, or he may read them like a musical score. But in any event we hope he will realize that the purpose of a definition is its service as a point of departure for individual thinking, and will question the definitions on the basis of his own experience with plays.

An *act* is a logical division of the play, marking a definite advance in the story and usually indicated objectively by the fall of the curtain.

Action is motivated movement.

An *antagonist* is a character who opposes most directly the protagonist, or main character, and is adversary to the propelling thought of the play.

Anticlimax is a term used to denote a moment of tension which comes after the climax, sometimes indicating a secondary climax and sometimes merely indicating a lessening of the effect of the climax.

The *apron* is the space on the stage in front of the curtain.

An *aside* is a confidential remark made by one character for the purpose of giving information to the audience and possibly to someone else on the stage, without informing all the participants upon the stage.

Atmosphere is the quality of a play that gives the illusion of locality and the harmony of mood.

A *ballet* is a theatrical form of dance which usually tells a story. See *Dance drama*.

The *basic situation* is the specific maladjustment from which the play arises.

A *burlesque* is a series of dramatic incidents depending primarily upon the use of extravagant images and upon contrast between subject matter and manner of treatment.

Business is a term used to indicate the obvious physical movement that takes place upon the stage for the purpose of revealing character, aiding action, or establishing mood.

A *cantata* is a story-poem set to music, with the major portion of the story carried by choral arrangements.

The *catastrophe* is an event of finality which forces a complete change of plan or intent.

Characterization is the bringing out of personality by means of setting, physical action, personal appearance, description, action, motivation, or by any other means.

The *chorus* is a group of chanters acting as a unit in the more or less passive role of interpreters of the play.

The *chronicle play* is one presenting historical characters with incidents chronologically arranged.

Classic tragedy is a term usually applied to the ancient Greek drama of heroic characters, lofty theme, and unity of action.

The *climax* of the play is the point of highest tension.

Closet drama, sometimes called literary drama, is drama written primarily to be read instead of acted.

Comedy shows character in action through such perspective that the incongruities of the situation touch the humor of the audience, and generally tends to show familiar characters in plausible situations, through them interpreting social conditions and ideas.

Comedy of intrigue depicts complications which arise from the placing of gay characters in irresponsible, nonconformist situations.

Comedy of manners presents sophisticated characters in a fairly plausible situation, satirizing foibles and artificialities of a period or class by the exaggeration of the situation and by witty lines.

Comic relief is the subordinate inclusion of comedy or even farce in a serious play in order to relieve emotional tension.

The *confidant(e)* is a character who receives the confidences of a central character. (The confidant is frequently, but not always, a "utility" character.)

Conflict denotes strife in which there is an element of doubt as to the outcome, a chance that the stronger force may, by exertion of will, modify the purpose or nature of the opposition.

A *crisis* in the play is an involvement which has to be modified before procedure is possible.

Curtain may mean either the physical curtain whose rise and fall separates a play into structural parts, or the curtain scene, in which case it is the last bit of action immediately preceding the fall of the curtain.

A dance drama is a story enacted mainly through dancing, whether in ballet or in modern dance.

The denouement is the moment when final suspense is satisfied, "the untying of the last knot."

Deus ex machina ("god from the machine") is a term used to indicate an act of fate which intervenes to save action from its logical consequence.

The development carries the play's main problem through a succession of stages each preparatory to the next, up to the point where resolution becomes a necessity.

Dialogue is the exchange of speech between or among characters. The expression "a dialogue" usually indicates only two participants.

A didactic play is one which has definite aim to instruct the mind or improve the morals.

Drama: literally "a doing." Upon the stage a drama is a representation of character in action.

A drame is a stirring play of serious theme, presenting characters in an arresting situation and developing a strong plot by emotional expectancy.

Elizabethan tragedy in general discarded the unities and departed from the use of classical myths, but kept the large central figure whose story made the play.

Entrance means not only a literal coming onto the stage, but the manner and effectiveness with which an actor comes onto the scene.

An epilogue is a final speech or scene after the action of the plot is finished.

An episode is a separate incident within the act.

The exciting force is the factor responsible for existing arrangements.

Exit is the leaving of the stage by one of the actors.

Exposition is the imparting of information necessary for an understanding of the story as it proceeds.

Expressionism is the representation of the subjective by means of the objective.

The extravaganza is a musical burlesque designed to produce its effect by humorous irregularity, overstatement of language, overdrawing of character, and overlauding of sentiment.

The *fantasy* is a romantic representation of the unlikely, the whimsical, the grotesque, without persuasion of reality.

Farce is that special brand of comedy in which logic of plot and development of character are subordinated to ludicrous situations for the purpose of exciting laughter.

Farce-comedy is a modern mingling of comedy characters in farce situations.

Foreshadowing is the indicating of action which may occur later in the play.

God from the machine: See *Deus ex machina.*

A *heroic comedy* is one in which a romantic central character carries the story adventurously and gallantly, meeting calamities with the philosophy of humor.

Impressionism is the substitution of transitory appearance for permanent fact—representational truth.

An *incident* is a happening, a subordinate but contributing part of an action.

The *inciting moment* is the instant at which some overt act upsets previous arrangements and thus makes the play go from balance to imbalance.

Inevitability is the unavoidable sequence of events growing out of character and the immutable law of circumstance.

The *initial situation* is the one with which the play opens.

The *interlude* is a light dramatic entertainment introduced between acts of a longer play.

Intrigue, comedy of: See *Comedy of intrigue.*

Irony in drama is a condition which is the reverse of what we have expected, or an expression whose intended implication is the opposite of its literal sense.

Light comedy presents a predominance of pleasant people in a pleasant situation with swift dialogue moving them toward some satisfactory end.

Literary drama: See *Closet drama.*

Liturgical drama is the drama of church ritual.

Manners, comedy of: See *Comedy of manners.*

The *masque* is a short, allegorical play in which the characters represent symbolical, mythical personalities.

Melodrama is a play which grows from situation with emphasis on the involvements of plot and the observance of certain romantic and moral standards.

The *miracle plays* were based upon the legends of the saints.

Modern dance: really a misnomer, the object of its original exponents having been to go back to primitive methods of expressing emotions per se, neither representationally nor narratively. Today, a term applied to a mode often combining elements of the new with the old to make a sort of theater dance with a dramatic modern accent. See *Dance drama*.

A *musical comedy* is a play which carries its story by spoken dialogue interspersed with songs and dances.

Music drama is a closely unified integration of drama and music, in which the dialogue is sung but not reiterated for musical effect. Sometimes spoken of as modern opera.

The *mysteries* were the dramatic representation of Scriptural events, particularly the mysteries of the Nativity, the Passion, and the Resurrection.

Naturalism is the literal transcription of reality.

Neoclassic tragedy was modeled after the Greek classic tragedy and adhered to the three "unities" of time, place, and action.

Obligatory scene: See *Scène-à-faire*.

An *obstacle* is anything—circumstance or character—which blocks at least temporarily an intended action.

An *opera* is an elaborate drama set to music.

Opéra bouffe is French comic opera, marked by buffoonery and burlesque, constructed on too light a scale to be ranked as *opéra comique*.

Opera buffa is the Italian opera of light, playful character built around a comic subject.

Operetta is a term which technically means a one-act opera but which is frequently used to designate almost any light opera.

An *oratorio* is a religious text set to music for solo voices, choruses, and instruments, and is presented without action, costumes, or scenery.

Pace means the speed of movement of a play.

A *pageant* is an elaborate pictorial presentation of narrative designed to give a unified total impression.

A *pantomime* is a play without words, a play of movements and attitudes.

Peripeteia, or peripety, is a reversal of circumstances which leads to a result contrary to expectation.

A *plant* is the apparently casual insertion of an idea, character, or property to be used more significantly later in the play.

Plausibility is the quality of apparent reasonableness in the presentation of character and circumstance.

A *play* is a story presented by actors on a stage before an audience.

Plot is the patterned arrangement of characters in a cumulative sequence of situations which unfold the story of the play.

Preparation denotes the previous arrangement of circumstances, the previous pointing of character, and the previous placing of properties so that ensuing actions and reactions may seem reasonable.

The *prologue* is an adjunct to the drama presented before the rise of the main story, standing outside the action and used for purposes of introduction.

A *propaganda play* is one whose purpose is to arouse an audience to thought and action.

The *proscenium arch* is the arch framing the curtain.

The *protagonist* in the play is the character who carries the main thought of the play.

Realism is representation without idealization.

Recognition is the discovery of a hitherto undiscovered character or fact.

Resolution is the procedure of solving the difficulties that have made the play.

Reversal is the accomplishment of an effect opposite to the effect intended by an action.

A *revue* is a melange of songs, sketches, dances, bound together chiefly by a topical interest.

Rhythm in the production of a play indicates a measured and apparently spontaneous flow of movement through which a unified impression is accomplished.

Romantic comedy is the comedy of chivalry and adventure.

Romantic tragedy, a term first applied to those tragedies which broke with the classic traditions, generally refers to the tragedy of personal adventure wherein the central characters die but leave our thoughts fixed upon the adventure rather than upon the fatal end.

Romanticism is the representation of the chivalrous and adventurous, the art of making the remote and improbable appear immediate and plausible.

A *satire* is a dramatic work which calls attention to follies or abuses by holding them up to rebuke through ridicule.

A *scenario* is the outline of the story of the play.

A *scene*, according to common use of the term in America, is a division of an act during which no change occurs in the presentation of time or place. It is also sometimes used synonymously with "setting." In the French use of the term a new scene occurs whenever a character exits or another character comes into the situation.

The scène-à-faire, or obligatory scene, is the scene that the playwright has led the audience to expect and without witnessing which they would feel disappointed if not cheated.

Sentimental comedy is the comedy of accepted standards presented in a romantic story with a happy ending.

A serious comedy is one which presents a thoughtful theme with characters fully realized, and generally treats these characters in a situation whose outcome is important in its social implications.

The setting of a play is literally its scene (in the sense of locale).

A situation is made up of characters in their relative positions within a temporary combination of circumstances.

A skit is a short dramatic episode usually satirical or humorous.

Social drama is the drama of protest, which questions customary attitudes toward problems of the day.

A soliloquy is a discourse in which the person addresses himself in tones designed to reach the audience.

The stage in terms of the modern physical theater is the elevated platform back of the proscenium arch.

The static play is one in which characters and situation are unchanged at the end of the play.

Struggle is an effort, frequently violent and labored, to meet or overcome an obstacle, differing from conflict in that sometimes the struggle is a "writhing" in the face of a foreknown doom.

Suspense is the sense of continuing uncertainty that gives drama its impetus.

A tableau is a vivid representation of a picture by a group of persons who remain motionless in appropriate postures.

The tag is the last line of a play.

Tempo is the timing of the play's movement.

Theater is that quality of the play which makes it peculiarly effective as it is produced before an audience.

The theme is the central thought of the play.

A tragedy is a play in which the individual battles with the universal to the inevitable catastrophe of the individual.

A tragicomedy is a play in which the implications of tragedy are averted by the introduction of comic incidents and a happy ending.

The *tragic flaw* is that factor in a character which weakens or intensifies in time of stress.

Unities is a term referring to the classic preference that a play should be represented as occurring within one day (unity of time), in one place (unity of place), and with no action irrelevant to the plot (unity of action).

Unity in the modern sense means unity of action achieved in a play's soundness of structure and story, its total impression of "wholeness" which gathers up plot, character, and dialogue within their frame of time and space so as to present a congruous picture.

A *utility character* is a character unnecessary to the plot but used to aid in exposition.

Vaudeville is a variety show composed of separate acts, loosely threaded together on a string of lively tunes.

The *well-made play* is a label applied to drama built to a precise pattern of structure, with situation, exposition, preparation, climax, and denouement deftly manipulated according to fixed laws of play construction.

Acknowledgments

The authors and publishers of this book acknowledge with appreciation the cooperation of the following publishers in granting permission to use copyrighted materials, as follows:

Quotations from the plays of James M. Barrie, reprinted by courtesy of Charles Scribner's Sons, New York.

Quotations from the plays of John Galsworthy, reprinted by courtesy of Charles Scribner's Sons, New York.

Quotations from the plays of George Kelly, reprinted by courtesy of Little, Brown and Company, Boston.

Quotations from Charles Rann Kennedy's *The Servant in the House*, reprinted by courtesy of Mr. Kennedy.

Quotations from W. Somerset Maugham's *The Circle*, reprinted by courtesy of Doubleday, Doran and Company, Inc., New York.

Quotations from Frank Hurburt O'Hara's *Today in American Drama*, reprinted by courtesy of The University of Chicago Press.

Quotations from the plays of Eugene O'Neill, reprinted by courtesy of Random House, Inc., New York.

Quotations from *Disraeli*, by Louis N. Parker, used by permission of the publishers, Dodd, Mead and Company, Inc., New York.

Quotations from *Riders to the Sea*, by John Millington Synge, reprinted by courtesy of John W. Luce and Company, Boston.

Quotations from *Lady Windermere's Fan*, by Oscar Wilde, reprinted by courtesy of Mr. Vyvyan Holland.

Index of Titles

Index of Names

Index of Subjects